Fast & Fresh
COOKING

Reader's Digest
Fast & Fresh Cooking

Inspired recipes
in minutes

Oded Schwartz &
Maddalena Bonino

Reader's
Digest

PUBLISHED BY THE READER'S DIGEST ASSOCIATION LIMITED
LONDON · NEW YORK · SYDNEY · CAPE TOWN · MONTREAL

A READER'S DIGEST BOOK

This edition published 1996 by Reader's Digest Association Limited
Berkeley Square House, Berkeley Square, London W1X 6AB

First published in Great Britain as
Fast & Fresh Vegetarian in 1994 by Oded Schwartz
Fast & Fresh Entertaining in 1994 by Maddalena Bonino
Fast & Fresh Mediterranean in 1995 by Oded Schwartz
by Kyle Cathie Limited
20 Vauxhall Bridge Road, London SW1V 2SA

ISBN 0276 422237 6

A Cataloguing in Publication record for this title is
available from the British Library

Photographs © Julie Dixon 1995, © Iain Bagwell 1994
© Michelle Garrett 1994
Illustrations © Sally Maltby 1994

Book Design by Tamasin Cole

Produced by Mandarin Offset Limited
Printed in Hong Kong

Contents

Acknowledgements

Food stylist for *Fast & Fresh Entertaining:* Liz Trigg

Food preparation and styling for *Fast & Fresh Vegetarian:* Oded Schwartz

Fast & Fresh Mediterranean would not have been possible without the help of the food conveyors of Finchley: Gary and his crew at Ellinghams, Andi at Ellenas, Pedro at P.S. Fisheries and Graham and David at Graham's Butchers. Thanks also to the Kasbah, Southampton Row, and to Selfridges for the loan of props.

A NOTE ON TIMING: Timings given for all recipes are approximate, as some people will work faster than others, and some recipes offer alternative methods which may take longer or shorter times. Timings for such tasks as cleaning fish – which you can ask your fishmonger to do for you – are given in brackets and not included in the total. Timings for each step within an individual recipe may not add up exactly to the total, as some steps can be carried out simultaneously (e.g. preparing vegetables while the pasta is cooking).

Introduction

Introduction

We all know the problem – on coming home from work there are hungry mouths to feed, perhaps friends coming to dinner, and what shall we cook? Of course we can pop to the nearest supermarket and buy bland ready made, convenience food or go out to eat at a characterless, fast food restaurant. Interesting food at good restaurants is an expensive choice, so it is worth cooking at home what our mothers called a real meal – nutritious, well balanced and delicious food that not only fills the stomach but also feeds the soul. Good food need not be difficult or time consuming to prepare, as this book proves. Using convenient, fast, modern equipment and time saving techniques, cooking is a joy.

The authors of this book share a passionate love of good food as well as a common origin – both were born, brought up and inspired by the sunny shores of the Mediterranean, the cradle of western cooking traditions; Maddalena Bonino comes from Italy and Oded Schwartz from Israel. The Mediterranean sun shines through the choice of recipes, which represent a varied and healthy cuisine that is easy and fun to cook. Inspiration is also drawn from other cultures, adopting exotic ingredients, new methods and different attitudes to food to create a selection of exciting dishes which reflect contemporary ideas and life styles.

The food presented here is robust, extremely tasty and very healthy. Based on the 'holy Trinity' – wheat, pulses and olive oil – with the addition of a wide variety of vegetables, fruit and fish, it contains all the elements required for a healthy diet. In moderation, the grape also benefits the healthy lifestyle and certainly enhances the conviviality of the region. Until recently meat was eaten very rarely and then only on weekends and holidays. Rearing animals was more important for their by-products – milk, cheese and butter – rather than for their meat and animals were therefore slaughtered only for special occasions such as a religious or domestic celebration or as a token of wealth. Even now, in many recipes, meat is used only as an additional ingredient to give extra flavour and texture to vegetables, grain and pulses. The recipes on the following pages reflect this and offer an exciting range of dishes based on the use of various grains – such as couscous, burgul, rice and maize – pasta and pulses. The Mediterranean regions are also blessed with a temperate climate – wet, cool winters and dry, sunny summers – an ideal hothouse for a vast range of fruit, vegetables and herbs. These are used in abundance – eaten fresh, in salads, used as a base for stews and casseroles, or cooked and served on their own.

Herbs are used profusely. Large quantities of culinary herbs, including parsley, fresh coriander, mint, spring onions, basil and oregano are used to add colour and flavour to many dishes and salads. Thyme, sage, rosemary, lavender and many more varieties are used not only to add flavour but also to preserve the dish – the thyme family contain a strong natural preservative, and are even used as a disinfectant and as a powerful remedy against bacterial stomach upsets. Bouquet garnis add flavour to many dishes. Although they differ according to recipe and locality, they usually contain thyme, rosemary, parsley, dill, celery and sometimes sage. When in season orange or lemon rind, or a citrus leaf freshly plucked from the garden, can be added to any dish to impart a note of freshness.

Cooking is a lot of fun, and the fun starts with shopping. Do not be afraid of some of the more exotic ingredients mentioned - shopping for them can be very rewarding. One of the greatest joys of cooking is buying fresh food. Walking around a well stocked market or even a supermarket inspires the cook – alternatives present themselves and new ingredients are discovered. Recently many of the larger supermarkets have started to sell wonderfully exotic vegetables and many specialised ethnic ingredients.

On your next shopping trip explore those enticing Aladdin's caves – the ethnic grocers. Don't be shy to ask for information, as enquiring about food is one of the greatest conversation starters, and even the surliest of grocers will smile and impart their knowledge.

The western mode of eating is historically tied to the three course meal – in other cultures this rigid division does not exist and the meal is made up of many small dishes. The recipes on the following pages provide the opportunity to experience a different way of eating. The best way to serve the dishes is in the form of a 'mezzah' – a buffet style meal in which a large variety of small dishes are served together and shared among the diners in a celebration of friendship and bonhomie.

The title Fast & Fresh should not mislead anyone into thinking that the recipes on the following pages are 'fresh' versions of 'fast food'. The preparation of food should not be hurried, although with practise any cook will acquire speed and, with a few hints on time saving techniques, many dishes can be assembled quickly. With that in mind most, if not all, the recipes in this book can be prepared in about 30 minutes, but don't be disappointed if it takes longer the first time you try one of them.

Also, remember that a well balanced meal does not need to be structured into three courses. Food is at its best when different dishes are shared among friends! Don't worry about food shopping and cooking – all will be well by simply using good, fresh ingredients, following the recipes and having fun.

Food for the Kitchen Cupboard

To make life easy and cooking fun, every cook should have a well stocked store cupboard. Select the best ingredients you can buy and store them in a cool, dry and dark place.

The following list are the basic ingredients which re-occur again and again in the book. But do not limit your store cupboard - whenever you are abroad or come across a new and wonderful ingredient, buy it and try it!

Oils: keep a few types of oil – a good extra virgin olive oil for dressing salads, sauces and other dishes, a less expensive, blender olive oil for cooking, a virgin nut and sesame oil for flavouring, and refined ground nut or sesame oil for recipes in which a flavourless oil is called for.

Sauces and relishes: Always have ready a few essential 'store' sauces, such as pesto, Moroccan harissa, salsa verde, soy and tahina paste. Home made or shop-bought, a tablespoon or two of these turns a dull dish into a delicacy.

Vinegars and souring agents: Keep a variety of vinegars – Balsamic or any other matured vinegars, such as raspberry or strawberry gives an instant, distinctive flavour to many salads, vegetable dishes and sauces. Lemons and limes are also useful for adding a fresh note. Tamarind, an eastern ingredient, will also come in handy. It can keep for years and only needs soaking to produce a superb fruity souring agent.

Onions, shallots and garlic: These three flavoursome bulbs lie at the heart of the Mediterranean cuisine. Raw, they supply texture and interest to salads or they can be eaten simply with bread, oil and salt. Cooked they impart colour, texture and flavour to soups and stews. They can be made into pickles, and there are even recipes for jams and confitures. Choose sound, dry bulbs without any blemishes, or sprout and store them in a cool dark place. Buy garlic in small quantities as it goes off very quickly in hot, humid kitchens. Shallots and onions are interchangeable, although shallots are used for a more subtle flavour and a crunchier texture.

Condiment: The store cupboard should always contain a couple of tins of anchovies, green and black olives, pickled gherkins, Moroccan pickled lemons, Italian sweet pickled peppers, pickled chillies and capers. All are used to give convenient and instant flavour to many dishes.

Tinned food: Some tinned food is excellent. Tinned pulses are ideal for adding to soups and salads. Tinned tomatoes are a wonderful standby when the only tomatoes available are the watery salad variety.

Nuts and seeds: Almonds, walnuts, peanuts, hazelnuts, pinenuts and chestnuts make wonderful bases for many sauces. Sesame seeds, poppy seeds and nigella seeds make interesting decorations, and add crunchiness and texture to many dishes. Keep a block of coconut cream to mellow hot dishes, and as a pleasant and versatile replacement for cream.

Dried ingredients: Keep dried mushrooms and sun dried tomatoes and various dried fruits, such as apricots, raisins and prunes. Rehydrated, in warm water, for 20 minutes or so they add superbly exotic flavour and sweetness.

Pastas: There is nothing quicker than cooking pasta – fresh pasta cooks in two to three minutes and dried, at the most, 12 minutes – for exact timing, check the instructions on the packet. There is a confusing array of pasta on the market and most of the varieties are interchangeable. Always store a few classic varieties and experiment with the new shapes which are constantly appearing in the shops.

Grain and grain products: The recipes in this book use a large variety of grains, as they have the advantages of keeping for a long time and being essential for a balanced diet. Store two kinds of rice – long grain basmati for pilaffs and short grain arborio for risotto. Other useful grains include couscous, the Moroccan staple which accompanies stews and can be added to salads; burgul, probably the most ancient convenience food and used all over the eastern Mediterranean, needing only soaking to be edible; and polenta, a wonderfully earthy meal of maze – the modern variety of which can be cooked in only five minutes.

Spices and herbs: Whenever possible, buy whole spices as they keep much longer. The most useful are black pepper, coriander, cumin, allspice, cloves, nutmeg, cardamom, turmeric, saffron and cinnamon.

Finally a word about herbs. Whenever possible, use fresh herbs; dried herbs, although convenient, have a different flavour. When using dried herbs remember to reduce the quantity as their flavour is more concentrated.

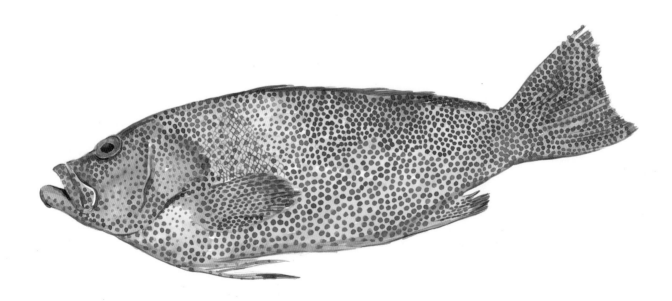

Time-Saving Tips

• One of the most time consuming aspects of cooking is peeling and chopping. Yet carrots, tomatoes, peppers, aubergines and many others, if fresh and sound, can and should be used unpeeled – just wash them thoroughly.

• Begin by following the recipes to the letter. The timing of the preparation is important and the recipes are devised to follow the most logical time table.

• Buy, if available, ready prepared ingredients if you want to save time. Although these are not at their best – as peeled and cut vegetables deteriorate very quickly – with the help of modern preservation techniques, some of them are satisfactory.

• Use tinned or frozen vegetables. Tinned tomatoes are sometimes preferable, especially when the alternative is the watery and tasteless 'salad' tomatoes.

• Chopping can be done with a food processor. Remember that the finer you chop foods, the quicker it cooks.

• Do not let chopped vegetables lie around, but use them as soon as you slice them. If you must leave cut vegetables waiting, sprinkle them with lemon juice to preserve their colour and slow down the deterioration process.

• To chill soups quickly, either plunge the container into a large bowl containing chipped ice and stir the soup frequently until cold or process with ice in a food processor. In this case remember that the soup is diluted by the ice and needs additional flavouring.

• Coriander and basil leaves are very tender and, when finely chopped, become a blackish green mass. They should either be snipped with scissors, sliced with a very sharp knife into a fine julienne, torn or roughly chopped.

• When preparing cold dishes ensure that your ingredients are as cold as possible to shorten cooling time.

The Recipes

SOUPS

AUBERGINE SOUP

30 minutes

Aubergines are not normally associated with soups but do try this recipe. It makes a delightfully piquant, pale pink soup. Serve with chunks of fresh bread and butter. Serves 4.

2 medium aubergines
3 tablespoons virgin olive oil
1 large onion, peeled & finely chopped
3 cloves of garlic, peeled & chopped
3 medium tomatoes, peeled, de-seeded & finely chopped
2 teaspoons tomato purée
1 litre/2 pints chicken stock
2 tablespoons lemon juice
salt & freshly ground black pepper

5

4 tablespoons basil leaves, roughly chopped

16-21

1 Heat oven to maximum 250°C/475°F/Gas Mark 9. With a fork, prick the aubergines in a few places and bake them for about 15-20 minutes or until very soft.

7-10

2 Heat the oil in a heavy-based pan, add the onion and garlic and fry over high heat for a few minutes or until the onion starts to change colour. Add the tomatoes, tomato purée, stock and lemon juice and bring to the boil. Reduce the heat and simmer for a few minutes.

5

3 When the aubergines are ready, remove from the oven, cut them in halves and scoop out the flesh carefully (they are very hot). Place in a food processor and process into a smooth purée.

3

4 Add the purée to the simmering soup and continue to simmer for a minute or two. Season with salt and pepper to taste. Add the basil and serve hot.
A tablespoon of thick cream could be stirred in just before serving.

CHESTNUT, MUSHROOM & ROCKET SOUP

The thought of cooking and peeling chestnuts may deter some people from trying this recipe. Fear not! You can find cooked and peeled chestnuts vacuum-packed in most supermarkets or good delicatessens! Serves 4.

30 minutes

350 g / 12 oz brown cap button mushrooms
50 g / 2 oz unsalted butter
2 tablespoons olive oil
1 medium onion, sliced
2 cloves of garlic, chopped
100 g / 4 oz chestnuts, cooked & peeled
1 litre / 1¾ pints hot vegetable stock or water
salt & freshly ground black pepper
2 tablespoons balsamic vinegar
50 g / 2 oz rocket leaves, cut into thin strips

8-10
1 tablespoon chopped flat-leaf parsley

2

1 Wash the mushrooms well and chop them roughly.

2 Heat two-thirds of the butter with the oil in a large saucepan. When they begin to sizzle, add the onion and garlic and fry for a few seconds. Then add the mushrooms and two-thirds of the chestnuts. Simmer for a couple of minutes, then add the stock or water.

4

10-15

3 Season and leave to cook for about 10-15 minutes.

4 Transfer to a food processor or liquidizer and whizz until smooth. Return to the pan and stir in the vinegar, rocket and parsley. Cover and keep hot.

2

5 Finely chop the remaining chestnuts. Melt the rest of the butter in a small pan and toss the chestnuts in it. Season well and fry until browned.

1

6 Serve the soup with the chopped chestnuts sprinkled on top, accompanied by crusty country bread.

1

COURGETTE & ROSEMARY SOUP WITH DITALINI PASTA

Ditalini is a pasta shape specially designed to be used in soups or broths. Look in any Italian deli for other such shapes. Serves 4.

25 minutes

100 g/4 oz ditalini pasta (small thimbles)
salt and freshly ground black pepper
3 tablespoons olive oil
1 medium onion, finely diced
1 clove of garlic, finely chopped
2 sprigs of fresh rosemary, washed & leaves removed
1 litre/1¾ pints hot vegetable stock or water
700 g/1½ lb courgettes, washed & thinly sliced
50 g/2 oz Parmesan cheese, freshly grated
2 tablespoons extra-virgin olive oil

10

6-8

1   First cook the pasta. Bring a large saucepan of salted water to the boil, drop in the ditalini and cook until just tender or *al dente*. Drain and rinse in cold water. Drain well again, then toss the pasta in 1 tablespoon of the olive oil to prevent it from sticking together. Set aside.

4-5

2   Heat the remaining olive oil in a large saucepan. Add the onion, garlic and rosemary and fry until the onion becomes transparent. Add in the stock or water and season well.

2-3

3   Bring to the boil, then drop in the courgettes. Return to the boil and cook for a couple of minutes, then add the cooked pasta.

1

4   Serve the soup sprinkled with the grated Parmesan and the extra-virgin olive oil.

SORREL & SPINACH BORSCHT

A refreshingly tart and delicious spring soup which can be served either hot or cold. The soup's origins are in Eastern Europe where it is served to celebrate the end of winter. The soup can be made entirely with spinach, in which case increase the vinegar to 75 ml/3 fl.oz or more to taste.

20-25 minutes

This soup is given its rustic quality and very special texture by leaving the sorrel whole or chopping it coarsely. If you prefer a smoother result just blend the soup in a blender, reheat and serve as suggested below. Serves 4.

225 g/8 oz sorrel, picked over & washed well in several changes of water, coarsely chopped or left whole
225 g/8 oz spinach, picked over & washed well in several changes of water, coarsely chopped or left whole

5

1 litre/2 pints vegetable stock or water

1 teaspoon salt
50 ml/2 fl.oz good white wine vinegar
1–2 tablespoons clear honey
100 ml/4 fl.oz soured cream

10

1 Put all the ingredients except the cream into a deep stainless-steel or enamel saucepan. Bring quickly to the boil, reduce the heat and simmer for 6–8 minutes, until the sorrel is tender.

2 Just before serving, stir in the cream. To prevent the cream from curdling, whisk it in a large tureen or bowl, add a ladle or two of soup and whisk well again. Add more soup and continue adding the soup until all is mixed. Serve immediately.

5

COURGETTE & POTATO SOUP

An elegant, pale green, refreshing summer soup which can be eaten warm (never hot) or cold. The courgettes are used unpeeled and grated on a coarse grater. When grating hold your courgette at a slant to achieve the longest strands possible – like short spaghetti. Try to serve the soup chilled with a dollop of soured cream or yogurt. Serves 4.

20 minutes

juice of 1–2 lemons
1 tablespoon sugar or clear honey (optional)
1 litre/2 pints pints stock or water
150 g/5 oz potatoes, peeled & sliced into 2.5-cm/1-in cubes

5

300 g/10 oz courgettes, coarsely grated
salt
2 tablespoons chopped fresh dill
soured cream or yogurt

1 Add the lemon juice and sugar or honey, if used, to the stock or water and bring to the boil. Add the potatoes, reduce the heat and simmer for about 15 minutes or until the potatoes are almost done. Add the courgettes and salt to taste, bring rapidly to the boil, boil for a minute or two, then remove from the heat. Allow to cool, add the dill and serve, either as it is, or with soured cream or yogurt.

15

QUICK BEETROOT BORSCHT

30 minutes

Although this recipe makes a good hot soup, it is best served cold, either as a starter or as a refreshing drink during or after a summer meal. For special occasions add to each serving a tot of vodka, gin or, even better, 50 ml/2 fl.oz chilled champagne. Serves 4.

1 kg/2¼ lb beetroot, peeled & roughly sliced
1.5 litres/3 pints vegetable stock or water
4 sticks of celery with their leaves, tied with string
juice of 1 or more lemons
1 tablespoon clear honey or sugar (optional)
1–2 tablespoons gherkin, finely chopped

5

soured cream, to serve

12

1 Put the diced beetroot into a food processor and process at high speed for 1 minute. Transfer to a deep stainless steel or enamel saucepan and add the stock or water. Add the celery and bring to the boil. Simmer over a moderate heat for 10 minutes.

10

2 Strain through a fine sieve and return to the pan. Add the lemon juice and honey, if used, and bring rapidly to the boil. Boil for a few seconds, then switch off the heat and skim. It can be eaten either hot or well chilled. Serve sprinkled with chopped gherkin and a dollop of soured cream.

NOTE: The very best accompaniment for hot soups is sherry or madeira.

QUICK TOMATO & PEPPER SOUP

30 minutes

This soup can be served either smooth or unsieved, for a grittier texture. Serves 4.

400 g/14 oz plum tomatoes
300 g/10 oz sweet red pepper, de-seeded & sliced
1 large onion, sliced
3 sticks of celery with leaves
1 litre/2 pints vegetable stock

5

juice of 1–2 oranges

a few drops of tabasco
salt
1 large orange, thinly sliced
100 g/4 oz Roquefort or Gorgonzola cheese,
  crumbled

20

1 Place the tomatoes, pepper, onion and celery in a food processor and process, starting and stopping the machine until finely chopped but not puréed. Transfer to a large saucepan, add the stock and bring to the boil. Reduce the heat to moderate and simmer for 15 minutes. For a smooth-textured soup, pass through a sieve or the fine blade of a food mill.

5

2 Return the soup to the rinsed saucepan. Add the orange juice, tabasco and salt to taste and bring to the boil, then reduce the heat to moderate and simmer for 1–2 minutes. Add the orange slices, keeping back a few to garnish, allow to simmer for a few seconds and turn off the heat.

1

3 Pour the soup into bowls. Float an orange slice topped with crumbled cheese on each and serve hot.

NOTE: Seville oranges, when in season, will add a wonderfully exotic flavour with a sour–bitter tang to the soup.

VEGETABLE SOUP WITH BARLEY & CHORIZO SAUSAGE

Chorizo is a delicious Spanish spicy sausage that can be eaten raw or cooked, and it's not unlike the Neapolitan 'salamella'. It is possible that while the Spanish governed southern Italy in the fifteenth and sixteenth centuries they left behind not only laws and taxes but a few recipes as well! Serves 4.

30 minutes

2 tablespoons olive oil
170 g/6 oz chorizo sausage, peeled & sliced
1 onion, peeled & diced
1 clove of garlic, chopped
1 carrot, peeled & diced
1 stick of celery, diced
1 small bulb of fennel, diced
1 courgette, diced
1 parsnip, peeled & diced

1 head of spring greens, sliced into strips
100 g/4 oz pearl barley, soaked in warm water for
    30 minutes
1 sprig of fresh thyme
3 bay leaves
1.4 litres/2½ pints hot vegetable stock or water
salt and freshly ground black pepper
1 tablespoon chopped flat-leaf parsley

10

3-4

1   Heat the oil in a large saucepan. Add the chorizo, onion and garlic and fry for a couple of minutes, then add all the vegetables one at a time, stirring well between each addition. Finally add the drained barley, thyme and bay leaves.

15-20

2   Add the stock or water, season and bring to the boil. Skim, then simmer for about 15–20 minutes.

1

3   Serve the soup piping hot, sprinkled with the parsley and accompanied by toasted ciabatta bread rubbed with garlic.

ROAST TOMATO SOUP SERVED WITH CHOPPED OLIVES, PEPPERS & EGG

30 minutes

700 g/1½ lb plum or firm beef tomatoes, washed &
    halved
1 medium red onion, roughly chopped
3 cloves of garlic, peeled
25 g/1 oz fresh ginger, peeled & grated
1 small bulb of fennel, roughly chopped
3 tablespoons olive oil
salt and freshly ground black pepper
400 ml/14 fl.oz hot vegetable stock or water
2 tablespoons balsamic vinegar

For the salsa
1 small red pepper, de-seeded & finely diced
8–10 basil leaves, chopped
1 hard-boiled egg, chopped
50 g/2 oz black olives, chopped
2 tablespoons extra-virgin olive oil

5

20

1   Place the tomatoes, onion, garlic, ginger and fennel in a roasting pan. Sprinkle with the olive oil, season and place in a pre-heated oven at 220°C/425°F/Gas Mark 7 for about 20 minutes, tossing from time to time until the vegetables are tender.

3

2   Remove from the oven, add the stock or water, sprinkle with the vinegar and liquidize in a blender. Adjust the seasoning and keep warm.

1

3   In a bowl mix the pepper, basil, egg and olives with 1 tablespoon of the extra-virgin olive oil. Season.

1

4   Serve the soup drizzled with the remaining extra-virgin olive oil and accompanied by the salsa.

PUMPKIN & TOMATO SOUP

30 minutes

A colourful and savoury autumn soup that can be served either as it is or creamed. Serves 4.

3 tablespoons olive oil
500 g/1 lb pumpkin, peeled & cubed
3 large tomatoes, peeled, de-seeded & chopped
1 large onion, peeled & finely chopped
2 green chillies, de-seeded & chopped (or more to taste)
1 litre/2 pints water or stock
1 teaspoon freshly ground coriander
salt
a few coriander leaves for decoration

5

5

1 Heat the oil in a large, heavy-based pan. Add all the vegetables and the ground coriander and fry over medium heat for about 5 minutes. Stir from time to time to mix and prevent scorching.

22

2 Add the liquid and bring to the boil. Skim, reduce the heat and simmer gently for about 20 minutes. Add the salt, sprinkle with coriander leaves and serve hot.

3

3 If you prefer a smooth finish, strain the soup and return the liquid to the cooking pot. Transfer the vegetables into a food processor and process, at high speed, into a smooth purée. Return to the pot, heat through and finish as above.

WINTER TOMATO SOUP

30 minutes

A satisfying and warming winter soup. Served with a chunk of bread and cheese, it makes a warming lunch dish. Serves 4.

3 tablespoons olive oil
1 teaspoon whole cumin
100 g/4 oz onion, chopped
3 cloves of garlic, peeled
1 kg/2 lb Italian tomatoes, sliced into large chunks
250 ml/8 fl.oz water
100 g/4 oz fresh breadcrumbs
juice of 1 orange
1 tablespoon chopped flat-leaf parsley or basil
salt & freshly ground black pepper

5

10

1 Heat the oil in a large, heavy-based pan. Add the cumin and fry for 2 minutes or until the cumin starts to pop and emits a pleasant roasted smell. Add the onion and garlic and fry until the onion starts to change colour. Add the tomatoes and the water and simmer for about 5 minutes.

15

2 Transfer to a food processor and process until smooth. Sieve the mixture into a clean pan, season with salt and pepper, add the orange juice and breadcrumbs and bring to the boil. Reduce the heat and simmer for about 10 minutes. Serve hot, sprinkled with chopped parsley or basil.

ONION SOUP WITH SMOKED CHICKEN & GRUYÈRE

A nice blend of strong flavours: more of a meal than a mere soup. Serves 4.

30 minutes

75 g/3 oz butter
1 tablespoon olive oil
350 g/12 oz onions, sliced
1 tablespoon brown sugar
1 tablespoon plain flour
1 teaspoon mustard powder
2 tablespoons dry white wine

2 tablespoons balsamic vinegar
1 litre/1¾ pints hot chicken stock
225 g/8 oz smoked chicken, boned & chopped
salt & freshly ground black pepper
75 g/3 oz Gruyère cheese, grated
2 tablespoons flat-leaf parsley, chopped

10

2-3

1 Heat the butter with the oil in a large saucepan. When they begin to sizzle, add the onions and fry until soft.

3-4

2 Add the sugar and leave to caramelize for a minute or two, stirring occasionally. Sprinkle in the flour and mustard and cook for a couple of minutes, then add the wine, vinegar and stock, stirring well.

6-7

3 Add the chicken, bring to the boil and season. Cook for a further 5 minutes. Serve the soup sprinkled with the Gruyère, chopped parsley and freshly ground black pepper, accompanied by plenty of crusty French bread.

SAVOY CABBAGE, SMOKED PANCETTA & POTATO SOUP

Definitely a soup for a cold day. Pancetta is Italian bacon; but I prefer the spicing and curing treatment my compatriots give to this widely used ingredient. Serves 4.

30 minutes

2 tablespoons olive oil
150 g/4 oz smoked pancetta or oak-smoked bacon
1 large potato, peeled & diced
1 medium onion, sliced
½ medium savoy cabbage, washed & cut into strips,
*   stalks & ribs removed*

zest of 1 orange, finely chopped
1 litre/1¾ pints hot vegetable stock or water
salt & freshly ground black pepper
75 g/3 oz mature Cheddar cheese, grated

7

4-5

1 Heat the oil in a large saucepan, then add the pancetta or bacon and leave to sizzle until almost crisp.

6-7

2 Add the potato and onion and fry briskly for a couple of minutes, then lower the heat and simmer for a further 5 minutes.

12-15

3 Add the cabbage, orange zest and stock or water. Bring to the boil, season and simmer for about 10 minutes until the potato is soft but the cabbage still slightly crunchy.

1-2

4 Serve the soup sprinkled with the grated Cheddar and freshly ground black pepper, accompanied by crusty bread.

GARLIC SOUP

The recipe is a version of the Provençal *soupe au pistou* **– a must for garlic lovers! This robust soup is from the African coast of the Mediterranean where it acquired its pungency. The amount of harissa below will give a pleasant hottish glow. Watch the frying garlic very closely as it tends to burn easily. Serves 4.**

30 minutes

2 tablespoons olive oil
1 large head of garlic, peeled & roughly chopped
3 medium potatoes, peeled & coarsely grated
3 medium tomatoes, peeled, de-seeded & coarsely grated
500 g/1 lb French beans, sliced into 2.5 cm/1 in lengths
1 litre/2 pints water or stock
75 g/3 oz vermicelli
salt & freshly ground black pepper

for the sauce
4 cloves of garlic, peeled
50 g/2 oz basil leaves
1 large tomato, peeled & de-seeded
1 tablespoon harissa or more (see page 257)
4 tablespoons of the soup

5

1 Heat the oil in a heavy-based pan, add the garlic and fry for 1 minute or until the garlic just starts to change colour. Add the potatoes, tomatoes and the beans, together with the liquid, and bring to the boil. Reduce the heat and simmer for 15 minutes. Add the vermicelli and the seasoning and cook for a further 5-8 minutes or until all is just tender.

25

2 To make the sauce put all the ingredients into a food processor and process into a smooth cream.

5

3 Stir the sauce into the soup, mix well and transfer into a heated tureen.

1

SPICY RED LENTIL SOUP WITH PARSLEY & LEMON YOGURT

30 minutes

Lentils with a difference. Red split lentils give this soup a wonderful 'creamy' texture. Delicious hot or warm. Serves 4.

50 g/2 oz unsalted butter
2 tablespoons olive oil
1 medium onion, sliced
2 cloves of garlic, chopped
½ teaspoon ground cumin
½ teaspoon ground coriander
1 small bulb of fennel, sliced
50 g/2 oz fresh ginger, peeled & grated
1 stick of lemon grass, sliced
1 small red chilli, de-seeded & chopped (optional)
1 litre/1¾ pints hot vegetable stock or water
300 g/10 oz red split lentils
salt & freshly ground black pepper
juice & grated rind of 1 lemon
1 tablespoon Greek-style yogurt
1 tablespoon chopped flat-leaf parsley

2

1 Heat the butter and oil in a large saucepan. When they begin to sizzle, add the onion, garlic, cumin and coriander and fry for a couple of minutes. Then add the fennel, ginger, lemon grass and chilli, if used. Add half the stock or water and cook for 10 minutes.

12

2 Add the lentils and the remaining stock or water, season and simmer for a further 10–15 minutes. Add the lemon juice and liquidize in a blender.

15

1

3 In a small bowl mix the yogurt and lemon rind with 1 tablespoon water. Add the parsley and season.

4 Serve the soup with a dollop of seasoned yogurt, accompanied by warm naan bread or warm buttered pitta bread.

1

RED LENTIL SOUP

This warming red soup is ideal for a cold winter night. Red lentils have a pleasantly mild, earthy flavour and when cooked turn golden-yellow. Those little lentils are also known as 'Egyptian lentils' and are reputed to be the ones used in the Biblical 'red pottage'. Split red lentils cook very fast and do not maintain their shape, resulting in a smooth pulp. If they are not too old and dry they will cook in less than 30 minutes, or less than 10 in a pressure cooker. Pre-soaking the lentils in water will also shorten the cooking time considerably. Serves 4.

45 minutes

150 g/5 oz split red lentils, well washed
1 litre/2 pints vegetable stock
1 large onion, sliced
4 cloves of garlic
1 large carrot, peeled & roughly chopped
2 tablespoons olive oil
2 teaspoons cumin seeds
3 medium tomatoes, peeled, de-seeded & roughly chopped
salt
4 tablespoons chopped fresh dill or coriander
1 small lemon, washed & sliced into thin rings
good olive oil, for sprinkling
sprigs of fresh dill or coriander, to garnish

5

1 Put the lentils into a large saucepan, cover with the stock and bring to the boil. Skim well, reduce the heat and simmer, half-covered, for 30 minutes.

30

2 Put the onion, garlic and carrot into the food processor and process at high speed, starting and stopping the machine until finely chopped but not puréed.

5

3 Heat the oil in a heavy-based frying pan. Add the cumin seeds and fry over a high heat until the seeds begin to pop. Add the chopped vegetables and continue frying for 5–8 minutes until they begin to brown. Add to the simmering soup, season to taste with salt and continue simmering until the lentils are tender.

10

4 Just before serving add the herbs and lemon slices, bring just to the boil and switch off the heat. Float a lemon slice on each serving, sprinkle with a few drops of olive oil and garnish with a sprig of dill or coriander.

1

NOTE: This soup is delicious gritty, but if a smoother texture is required, strain it through a sieve, reserving the liquid. Put the contents of the sieve into a food processor and process at high speed for 1 minute. Return to the pan together with the cooking liquid and bring to the boil. Simmer for 2–3 minutes and finish as above.

WHITE FOAM SOUP

30 minutes

This curious Spanish soup has an extraordinary texture, that of a very soft and velvety cheese soufflé. Use a good mature cheese such as hard mountain Spanish or cheddar. Serves 4.

25 g / 1 oz butter
1 onion, peeled & chopped
2 cloves of garlic, peeled & crushed
1 stick celery, chopped
½ tablespoon flour
1 litre / 2 pints milk
1 blade of mace (or ½ a nutmeg)
2 eggs
50 g / 2 oz grated cheese
salt & freshly ground black pepper
1 tablespoon chopped parsley
4 tablespoons garlic croûtons

5

2

1 Melt the butter in a heavy-based pan, add the onion, garlic and celery and fry for a few moments.

2 Sprinkle with the flour and continue to fry for a minute or two. Add the milk and the mace, bring to the boil, reduce the heat and simmer for 15 minutes.

20

3

3 In the meantime separate the eggs and beat the whites into a stiff snow.

4 Remove the pot from the heat and allow to cool for a minute or two. Beat the yolks and add to the pot together with the cheese. Mix well and fold in half the egg white. Return to the heat and re-heat, being careful never to let the soup boil.

2

5 Transfer the rest of the egg white to a heated soup tureen and pour over the hot soup. Serve immediately, sprinkled with chopped parsley and well-flavoured garlic croûtons.

1

CUMIN SOUP

30 minutes

The recipe is based on a Tunisian one normally made from dried broad beans. I have replaced the beans with leeks, which make an ideal background to the cumin – the dominating flavour of this soup. Serves 4.

2 tablespoons virgin olive oil
1 teaspoon whole cumin seeds
750 g / 1½ lb leeks, trimmed, washed & thinly sliced
2 cloves of garlic, peeled & mashed
3 medium potatoes, peeled & coarsely grated
2-3 merguez sausages, dry chorizo or spicy kabanos
2 teaspoons harissa
1 litre / 2 pints water or stock
salt

5

3

1 Heat the oil in a heavy-based pan, add the cumin and fry for a minute or two until the seeds start to pop.

2 Add the rest of the ingredients and bring rapidly to the boil. Skim, reduce the heat and simmer for 15-20 minutes. Taste for seasoning. Serve hot.

22

POTATO & CARROT SOUP

A substantial and delicious Central European soup which is particularly good on a cold winter evening. Served with a chunk of fresh bread, cheese and salad, it makes a quick and nourishing meal. The soup can be made richer with the addition of 100 ml/4 fl.oz double cream replacing some of the water. Serves 4.

35 minutes

50 g/2 oz butter
2 heaped teaspoons roasted caraway seeds
2 medium onions, peeled & chopped
200 g/7 oz carrots, peeled & cubed
500 g/1 lb 2 oz potatoes, peeled & cubed
600 ml/1 pint milk
600 ml/1 pint water
1 tablespoon oats or rice
salt & freshly ground black pepper
75 g/3 oz Gruyère cheese, grated
5 *finely chopped fresh parsley*

6-7 1 Heat the butter in a large, heavy-based saucepan. Add the caraway seeds and fry for about 1 minute on a moderate heat or until the seeds start to pop. Then add the onions and carrots and fry for about 5 minutes or until the mixture begins to take colour.

20 2 Add the potatoes, the milk, water, and the oats. Season to taste. Bring to the boil, then simmer for about 20 minutes, until the potatoes are tender. Serve hot, sprinkled with the cheese and parsley.

TARATOR

The origin of this soup is Bulgaria. The name 'tarator' is probably misleading as around the Eastern Mediterranean it implies a sauce. Whatever, the soup is a refreshing summer starter made in less than 15 minutes. Serves 4.

15 minutes

600 ml/1 pint Greek yogurt
grated rind & juice of 1 lemon
3 tablespoons chopped fresh dill or mint, or both
75 ml/3 fl.oz olive oil
salt
1 small onion
1–2 cloves of garlic
350 g/12 oz cucumber, coarsely chopped
5 *15–20 ice cubes*

2-3 1 In a large bowl beat together the yogurt, lemon rind and juice, herbs, olive oil and salt to taste.

3 2 Put the onion, garlic and cucumber into a food processor and process at high speed, starting and stopping the machine until the vegetables are finely chopped but not puréed. Add to the yogurt mixture.

2-3 3 Put the ice cubes into the processor and process to a slash. Add to the yogurt and cucumber mixture. Decorate with sprigs of mint and serve.

OKRA SOUP

Okra is a versatile vegetable with a wonderful earthy flavour and an interesting texture. Cooked one way it supplies a smooth, almost velvety finish to soups and stews, cooked another it can be served as a deliciously crunchy salad. Okra is available almost all year round in Greek, Mediterranean and Indian grocers. It is also available in some supermarkets.

Select young, fresh, intensely green pods the ends of which should snap off crisply. Avoid yellowed limp pods that are tough and stringy. To prepare the okra remove the hard stem and wash well. Serves 4.

30 minutes

4 tablespoons virgin olive oil
150 g/6 oz leek, finely chopped
2 medium tomatoes, peeled, de-seeded & chopped
1 tablespoon tomato purée
1 litre/2 pints chicken or vegetable stock
250 g/8 oz young okra, trimmed & sliced into 2.5 cm/1 in slices
2 tablespoons lemon juice
salt
chopped parsley

7

5

1 Heat 2 tablespoons of the oil in a large, heavy-based pan and add the okra. Fry over a high heat until the okra starts to brown. Lift out the okra and drain on absorbent kitchen roll.

2 Heat the rest of the oil. Add the leeks and fry, over high heat, for a minute or two or until the leek becomes transparent. Stir in the tomatoes, tomato purée and the stock and bring to the boil. Reduce the heat and simmer for 10 minutes or until the okra is tender.

15

3

3 Season with lemon and salt just before serving. Serve hot decorated with chopped parsley.

COLD ALMOND SOUP

The following soup is a direct descendent of a medieval Spanish recipe, and surprisingly makes a delicious and different summer soup. It tastes wonderful with roasted almonds, but although the flavour is superb, the beige colour of the soup might put people off. Add a few drops of natural bitter almond essence to intensify the almond flavour. Serves 4.

15 minutes

150 g/6 oz almonds, blanched & peeled
100 g/4 oz bread, crustless, soaked in cold water
2 cloves of garlic
6 ice cubes
4 tablespoons good olive oil
juice of 1 lemon
salt
500 ml/1 pint very cold chicken stock or water
100 g/4 oz cucumber, chopped
100 g/4 oz apple, chopped

5

4 sprigs of mint

5

1 Place the almonds in the food processor and process, at high speed, until the almonds are powdered. Squeeze the bread to exude as much moisture as possible and add to the almonds together with the garlic, ice cubes, lemon juice, zest and salt and process to a smooth cream.

5

2 With the machine still running, gradually add the oil. Transfer the mixture into a large serving bowl, add the stock and mix well. Adjust the seasoning and serve, very cold, decorated with some of the chopped apples and cucumber and a sprig of mint. The rest of the chopped cucumber and apple is sent to the table separately so diners can help themselves.

5

CHERRY SOUP

A delightful cold summer soup originating from Hungary. The soup can be made all year round using tinned sour cherries. The most suitable cherries to use are sour varieties such as Morellos or Amarelles. Removing the stones from the cherries can be a laborious job without a cherry stoner. This small, ingenious and inexpensive device can be found in many kitchen equipment shops. Serves 4.

25 minutes

750 g / 1 lb 10 oz Morellos cherries, washed & stoned
1 litre / 2 pints vegetable stock or water
2–3 tablespoons clear honey
1 cinnamon stick
1 tablespoon cornflour
½ teaspoon salt
2 tablespoons lemon juice
zest of 1 lemon, cut into fine julienne strips
75 ml / 3 fl.oz port or dry red wine, chilled

5

150 ml / 5 fl.oz whipping cream

10

1   Put the cherries into a large stainless steel or enamel saucepan. Add the stock or water, honey and cinnamon. Bring to the boil, then simmer for about 5 minutes.

5-7

2   Mix the cornflour with the salt, lemon juice and a little water, if needed, and add to the simmering soup. Simmer for a few more minutes, then add the lemon zest and remove from the heat. Allow to cool completely, then chill well.

3   ·

3   Just before serving add the port or wine. Swirl some cream on each portion and serve.

NOTE: To chill soups quickly either plunge the bowl into a larger bowl containing chipped ice and mix frequently until cold, or process with ice in a food processor. In this case, remember that the soup will be diluted by the ice and will need additional flavouring.

FRESH SWEETCORN, SUN-DRIED TOMATOES & SMOKED HADDOCK CHOWDER

30 minutes

Chowders usually combine meat and fish. In this case the sun-dried tomatoes substitute the meat. Serves 6–8 as a soup, 4 as a meal.

75 g/3 oz unsalted butter
1 medium bulb of fennel, sliced
1 large potato, peeled & diced
1 medium onion, sliced
1 clove of garlic, chopped
2 small leeks, sliced
6 sun-dried tomatoes, thinly sliced
100 g/4 oz baby sweetcorn, sliced
zest of 1 lemon, finely chopped
1.4 litres/2½ pints warm milk
225 g/8 oz smoked undyed haddock, skinned &
    bones removed
salt & freshly ground black pepper
1 small red chilli, de-seeded & finely sliced (optional)
3 tablespoons chopped flat-leaf parsley

8-10

4

1   Melt the butter in a large saucepan. Add the fennel, potato and onion and simmer for a few minutes. Add the garlic, leeks, sun-dried tomatoes, sweetcorn and lemon zest.

10-15

2   Pour in the milk and bring to the boil. Skim, then simmer for about 10 minutes until the potatoes are soft.

2-3

3   Cut the haddock into rough pieces. Add to the pan, season with plenty of pepper and add the chilli, if used.

6-7

4   Return to the boil, skim again if necessary, and check the seasoning. Stir in the parsley, cover and leave to stand for 5 minutes. Serve the soup with toasted bread.

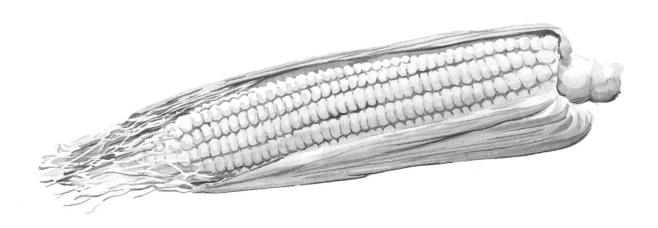

CLEAR FISH SOUP WITH SQUID, PRAWNS & MUSSELS

A fragrant and refreshing soup. Try different combinations of fish and shellfish with the basic stock. Serves 4.

20 minutes

- 1 litre/1¾ pints water
- 2 tablespoons soy sauce
- 2 tablespoons sake
- 1 teaspoon wasabi (Japanese horseradish)
- 2 sticks of lemon grass, thinly sliced
- 25 g/1 oz fresh ginger, cut into thin strips
- 5 coriander stalks, leaves removed & reserved
- 1 small red chilli, seeds removed & cut into strips (optional)
- 20 mussels, shells scrubbed & 'beards' removed
- 100 g/4 oz baby squid, cleaned & cut into thin strips
- 100 g/4 oz prawns, cooked & peeled
- 1 red pepper, cut into thin strips
- 1 spring onion, thinly sliced
- 1 medium carrot, cut into thin strips
- 50 g/2 oz fine bean shoots

5-8

- salt & freshly ground black pepper

2-3

1 First make the stock. Bringing the water to the boil in a large saucepan with the soy sauce, sake, wasabi, lemon grass, ginger, coriander stalks and chilli, if used.

2 Cook the mussels: heat a heavy-based saucepan, and when hot put in the mussels and cover with a tight-fitting lid. Holding the lid down firmly, shake the pan two or three times. The intense heat will make the mussels spring open in a few minutes. When all the mussels are open, remove from the heat, drain and keep warm. Discard any that do not open.

8-10

3 Place the squid, prawns and cooked mussels in a large serving bowl or individual bowls with the pepper, spring onion, carrot and bean shoots. Season then pour the piping hot stock over, garnish with the reserved coriander leaves and enjoy!

5

HOT & SOUR SOUP

30 minutes

One of the great soups of South-East Asia. Light, hot and sour, it makes an ideal starter to a rich dinner. Serves 4.

2 tablespoons light sesame oil
4 shallots, finely chopped
3 cloves of garlic, finely chopped
2 small red or green chillies, thinly sliced into rings
5-cm/2-in stick of lemon grass, finely chopped
100 g/4 oz oyster mushrooms, broken into large chunks
75 g/3 oz shitake mushrooms, stems removed & thinly sliced
1 litre/2 pints vegetable stock
5 tablespoons rice or white wine vinegar
salt
1 tablespoon chopped fresh coriander

5

1   Heat the oil in a large saucepan. Add the shallots and the garlic and fry over a high heat until the shallots begin to change colour. Add the chillies and lemon grass and fry for about 4–5 minutes or until all are nicely browned.

10

2   Add all the remaining ingredients except the coriander and simmer gently for 15 minutes. Add the coriander and serve immediately.

15

NOTE: Coriander and basil leaves are very tender and when chopped finely result in a blackish green mass. They should either be snipped with scissors, sliced with a very sharp knife into fine julienne strips, or torn or chopped roughly.

TUSCAN BEAN SOUP WITH PESTO

Bean soups are delicious 'the day after', so if you have any left over try re-heating it in a warm oven in an ovenproof dish, drizzled with olive oil and covered with thin slices of onion. The Tuscans call this 'ribollita' (reboiled). Serves 6–8 as a soup, 4 as a meal

30 minutes

2 tablespoons olive oil
50 g/2 oz lean pancetta, cut into small cubes
1 medium onion, diced
1 clove of garlic, chopped
1 carrot, peeled & diced
2 sticks of celery, diced
1 medium leek, diced
75 g/3 oz savoy cabbage, cut into thin strips
200 g/7 oz cannellini beans, cooked, washed & drained

200 g/7 oz borlotti beans, cooked, washed & drained
1 large ripe tomato, diced
1 sprig of fresh rosemary
1 sprig of fresh thyme
1.4 litres/2½ pints hot vegetable stock or water
salt & freshly ground black pepper
4 slices of day-old country-style bread
1 clove of garlic, halved
4 tablespoons pesto (see below)

4-5

1   Heat the oil in a large saucepan. Add the pancetta and fry for a few minutes, then add the onion, chopped garlic, carrot, celery, leek and cabbage. Leave to sizzle for a couple of minutes, then add the beans, tomato and herbs. Add the stock or water and season.

5

15-20

2   Bring to the boil, then simmer for 15–20 minutes.

1

3   Meanwhile, toast the slices of bread and rub with the cut garlic. Place a slice at the bottom of each serving bowl, pour over the hot soup and serve with a dollop of pesto.

PESTO

100 g/4 oz pine-nuts
2 cloves of garlic, peeled
a large bunch of basil
100 ml/3½ fl.oz olive oil
100 ml/3½ fl.oz extra-virgin olive oil
75 g/3 oz Parmesan cheese, freshly grated
salt and freshly ground black pepper

2

1   Place the pine-nuts, garlic and basil in a food processor, and whizz to obtain a well-blended paste. Then pour in the two oils while the machine is still running. Scrape the pesto out of the processor and blend in the Parmesan. Check the seasoning and use as required.

3

NOTE: When you make pesto, make more than you need for the recipe. Pesto improves by 'standing' in the fridge. Just pour the excess into a jar, screw the lid on tightly and use when required.

Tuscan Bean Soup with Pesto,
and Fresh Sweetcorn, Sun-dried Tomatoes
& Smoked Haddock Chowder
(page 43)

MUSHROOM & CORIANDER SOUP

30 minutes

This delicious savoury soup is made using a recipe discovered in Israel. The combination of mushroom and coriander is magical and the colour is wonderfully green and appetizing. Serves 4.

3 tablespoons olive oil
1 large onion, finely chopped
400 g/14 oz mushrooms, sliced
1 litre/2 pints vegetable stock
1 large bunch of fresh coriander, stems removed & leaves coarsely chopped
juice of 1 lemon
salt & freshly ground black pepper
soured or double cream (optional)

10

15

1 Heat the oil in a large saucepan. Add the onion and fry gently for about 5 minutes or until the onion is transparent. Add the mushrooms and continue to fry until they begin to emit their liquid. Add the stock, bring to the boil and simmer gently for about 10 minutes.

3-5

2 Add the coriander and lemon juice, and season to taste, then bring to the boil and boil for 2 minutes. Serve hot, with or without a dish of soured cream.

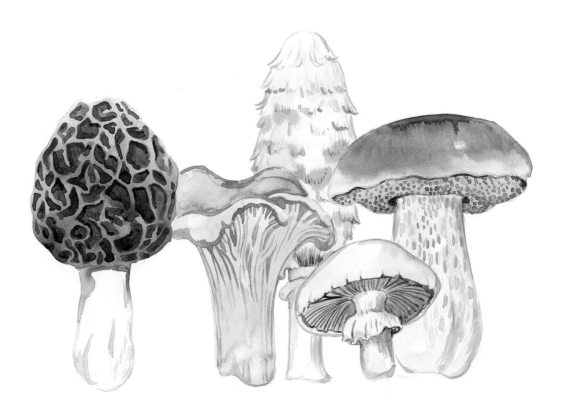

BEANS & SPINACH SOUP

30+ minutes

A colourful and wonderfully satisfying winter soup. Use either spinach, winter greens or the flashy, earthy leaves of silver beet. Serves 4.

4 fat cloves of garlic finely chopped
2 medium onions, peeled & coarsely chopped
300 g/12 oz spinach, washed
1 litre/2 pints chicken or vegetarian stock
400 g/14 oz cannelloni or butter beans
juice of 1 large lemon
salt to season
1 teaspoon whole cumin seeds

10

2 tablespoons fresh coriander leaves for decoration

5

1   Heat the oil in a heavy-based pan. Add the garlic and onion and fry for a few minutes, or until the onion starts to change colour.

2   Place the washed spinach into a food processor and process, starting and stopping the machine until the mixture is finely chopped but not puréed. Add to the pan and fry over a high heat until the spinach is wilted. Add the stock and beans. Bring to the boil and simmer for about 15 minutes. Add the lemon juice, salt and cumin; mix well. Decorate with coriander leaves and serve either hot or warm.

17

STARTERS

SPINACH & FETA CHEESE PIE

This simple and quick pie can be served either hot or at room temperature. Take time to clean the fresh spinach thoroughly. Alternatively use chopped frozen spinach.

Filo pastry is available in many supermarkets and can be bought easily either fresh or frozen. Remember the filo dries very quickly and when waiting to be used should be always covered with a slightly dampened cloth. Serves 4.

30 minutes

750 g/1½ lb fresh spinach blanched or 500 g/1 lb frozen spinach, roughly chopped
250 g/8 oz feta cheese, coarsely grated
2 eggs plus 1 egg white, lightly beaten
50 g/2 oz flaked almonds or pine-nuts which have been previously browned in a little oil
salt & freshly ground black pepper and a few gratings of nutmeg
10 sheets of filo pastry
4-5 tablespoons olive oil for brushing
1 egg yolk, well beaten together with a pinch of salt & a tablespoon of water

5

sesame or nigella seeds (optional)

1

1 Pre-heat the oven to 200°C/400°F/Gas Mark 6.

2 To blanch the spinach, first prepare a large bowl with very cold water. Then fill a large pan with water and 2 teaspoons of salt. Bring to a rapid boil and add half the amount of spinach. Bring back to the boil and then with the help of a slotted spoon or a skimmer remove the spinach directly into the cold water. Repeat with the other half of the spinach. Strain the spinach and gently squeeze it between your hands to exude as much

7

moisture as possible.

5

3 In a large bowl mix the spinach with the feta cheese, eggs, and egg white, almonds and seasoning.

4 Brush a suitable ovenproof dish with oil and cover the bottom and sides with four sheets of filo pastry, brushing each thoroughly with the oil. Cover them with an even layer of spinach filling. Add another layer of filo, followed by more spinach mixture and finally top with the remaining sheets of filo, brushing each layer with the oil. Trim and tuck in any loose edges, brush with the egg yolk mixture and sprinkle with sesame or

5

nigella seeds.

15-20

5 Bake in the oven for 15-20 minutes or until the crust is crisp and golden.

AUBERGINE & FETA CHEESE 'GÂTEAU'
SERVED WITH FRESH TOMATO SAUCE

Aubergine is a favourite vegetable for many recipes. But people often think it does not have any flavour! Yet its blandness makes it a splendid carrier of flavours. Aubergine has another unique quality: if fried or grilled, its flesh has a texture resembling that of tender meat; when baked or roasted whole it acquires a smooth, velvety texture.

In the following recipe the aubergine can either be grilled or gently fried in olive oil. When fried, aubergine tends to soak up a lot of oil. To prevent this, salt the sliced aubergine and leave for 30 minutes, then drain and pat dry. Always drain fried aubergines on kitchen paper.

The simplest way to serve aubergine is to roast it whole on an open fire, turning it from time to time until the skin is evenly charred and the flesh inside is very soft. Or you can bake it in a very hot oven for 20 minutes, then scoop out and mash the pulp and flavour with chopped onion, garlic, lemon juice, salt and olive oil. Serve immediately. Serves 4.

30 minutes

2 large, long aubergines
olive oil, for brushing
220 g/8 oz feta cheese, coarsely grated
Fresh Tomato Sauce (see pages 267), flavoured with 2 tablespoons coarsely chopped fresh basil, to serve
3-5
sprigs of fresh basil, to garnish

1

1 Heat the grill.

2 Trim the aubergines and slice them lengthways into 8 mm/⅓ in slices. Brush each slice generously with oil. Grill under the hot grill for 4–5 minutes on each side or until the aubergine is cooked and golden-brown. Keep
20-25   warm while grilling the remaining aubergine slices.

3-5   3 Allow 3 slices per portion. Sandwich them together with layers of feta cheese.

4 To serve, put each 'gâteau' on a plate. Pour the sauce over the corner of the gâteau so that some of the sauce
5   remains on top and the rest creates an appetizing pool around it. Garnish with a sprig of basil.

Aubergine & Feta Cheese 'Gateau'
served with Fresh Tomato Sauce (page 267)
and Stuffed Squash (page 198)

DEEP FRIED AUBERGINE

These light and crisp fritters are best done just before serving. Other vegetables such as courgettes, courgette flowers, potatoes, carrots, cauliflower, broccoli or young, tender artichokes can be fried in the same way.

Serve with a dip as a snack or on a pool of sauce such as tahina (see page 257) or tarama (see page 79) as a delicious first course. Serves 4.

30+ minutes

100 g/4 oz plain flour
250 ml/8 fl.oz very cold beer or sparkling water
2 tablespoons sesame seeds
1 tablespoon chopped fresh (or 2 teaspoons dry) thyme, savory or tarragon
2 medium aubergines sliced into rounds and then into 1.5 cm/½ in 'chips'
ground nut or sesame oil for deep frying

5

salt

17-20

1 First make the batter. Whisk the flour into the cold beer and add the sesame and herbs and mix well. Allow the mixture to stand in the fridge, covered, for at least 15 minutes.

10

2 Heat the oil until it is steaming. Drop a few aubergine 'chips' into the cold batter and then into the hot oil and fry for 3-4 minutes until the chips are crisp and golden. Drain well on absorbent paper. Sprinkle with salt and serve hot on a pool of the chosen sauce.

CHARD OR SPINACH MILLE-FEUILLE

This elegant first course calls for chard, also known as silver beet or just beet. It can be bought from most Indian, oriental and Middle Eastern grocers. The leaves are fairly large and have a wonderfully earthy flavour. If unavailable, use spinach instead.

Filo pastry can be bought fresh from delicatessens and is readily available frozen from supermarkets. Remember that the pastry dries very quickly and when waiting to be used should always be covered with a slightly dampened cloth. Serves 4.

35 minutes

50 g/2 oz butter, melted
4 tablespoons olive oil
8 sheets of filo pastry
1 large onion, finely chopped
1 clove of garlic, finely chopped
1 small chilli, cut into thin rings (optional)
500 g/1 lb 2 oz chard or spinach leaves, washed, trimmed & cut into narrow strips
juice of 1 orange
3 strips of orange zest, cut into fine julienne strips
freshly grated nutmeg
salt

10

½ quantity of Yogurttese (see page 259), flavoured with 1 tablespoon chopped fresh tarragon, to serve

1

1   Heat the oven to 200°C/400°F/Gas Mark 6.

2   Mix the melted butter with 1 tablespoon oil and use to brush each sheet of filo lightly, arranging the sheets on top of each other in groups of four. Cut each group lengthwise into 3 equal wide strips and cut each strip into 2, creating 6 rectangles. Lay each on a silicon-lined baking tray. Bake in the pre-heated oven for 10–12 minutes or until crisp and golden. Keep warm.

15-20

3   Heat the remaining oil in a large frying pan. Add the onion, garlic and chilli, if used, and fry over a high heat for a few minutes until the onion is translucent. Add the chard or spinach and continue frying until it is limp. Add the orange juice, zest, nutmeg and salt and continue cooking until almost all the liquid has evaporated.

6-8

4   Sandwich the cooked chard or spinach between 2 filo squares, return to the baking tray and reheat thoroughly in the oven. Serve hot on a pool of tarragon-flavoured Yogurttese.

5

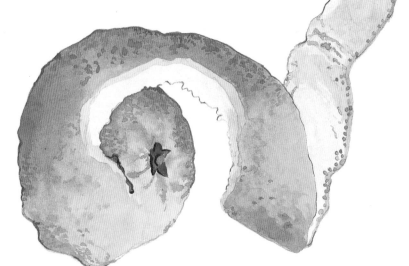

CARROT CUSTARDS

The recipe for these delicate custards is based on a dish by Michel Guerard, the father of the important, but short-lived, *cuisine minceur*. They are light and fragrant and contain very few calories. I sometimes vary their flavour by adding a 25 cm/1 in piece of fresh ginger, peeled and finely chopped, instead of the coriander. Serves 4.

35 minutes

butter & ground almonds or breadcrumbs, for coating
500 g/1 lb 2 oz carrots, peeled & coarsely chopped
200 g/7 oz fromage frais or Quark
1 tablespoon clear honey
3 eggs (size 3)
1 teaspoon ground coriander
salt & freshly ground black pepper
100 g/4 oz highly matured Cheddar cheese, grated
1 tablespoon chopped fresh coriander leaves
a bunch of watercress & coriander leaves, to garnish
½ quantity of Yogurttese (see page 13), flavoured with 1 tablespoon fresh coriander leaves,
    cut into fine julienne strips, to serve

5

1

1 Heat the oven to 220°C/425°F/Gas Mark 7. Butter 6 ramekins well and sprinkle with ground almonds or breadcrumbs.

2 Put the carrots into a food processor and process at high speed for 1 minute or until the carrots are almost puréed. Add the fromage frais or Quark, the honey, eggs, ground coriander, salt and pepper and process until well amalgamated. Fold in the grated cheese and the chopped coriander.

3-4

3 Pour the mixture into the prepared ramekins and cover each with a piece of silver foil. Arrange the ramekins in a roasting pan and pour in boiling water to come halfway up the sides of the ramekins. Bake in the pre-heated oven for 20 minutes.

2-2

4 Allow the ramekins to rest for a few minutes. Loosen the sides with a small knife and unmould, with a sharp tap, on to a serving plate. Arrange a few watercress leaves around one side of the custard and spoon some Yogurttese sauce on the other. Decorate the top of each custard with a coriander leaf and serve.

3-5

STEAMED VEGETABLE CUSTARDS

A light and elegant dish which comes from Japan. It is ideal as a starter for a substantial meal such as Christmas dinner. Served with a fresh, crisp salad dressed with sesame oil it makes a wonderful summer lunch dish. Serves 4.

30 minutes

75 g/3 oz petits pois
1 small carrot, peeled & sliced into 2 mm/⅛ in rings
100 g/4 oz baby spinach leaves, blanched or steamed
6 small shitake mushrooms, stems removed & thinly sliced
2 tablespoons snipped chives or the green parts of 2 spring onions
600 ml/1 pint vegetable stock or water
2 tablespoons sake or very dry sherry
2 tablespoons light soy sauce
2.5 cm/1 in stick of lemon grass, finely chopped

5

5 eggs (size 3)

5

1   Toss all the vegetables together with the chives and divide among 6 well-buttered ramekins or coffee cups. Mix the stock or water, sake or sherry, soy sauce, lemon grass and eggs and beat well. Pour over the vegetables.

10-20

2   Place the ramekins or cups in a large steamer and steam for 10–20 minutes or until a wooden cocktail stick inserted into the custard comes out clean. Serve hot, in its mould.

BROAD BEANS SERVED WITH YOGURT

There is an amazing variety of fresh legumes available in markets around the Mediterranean. Beans come in a fantastic range of shapes, sizes and colours, and can be used in an equally vast range of salads, first courses, meat stews and soups. This Turkish recipe is a delicious combination of the earthy flavour of broad beans with tart, refreshing and minty yogurt sauce. Shelling broad beans is labour intensive; it is the stuff of family mythology – long summer evenings and children quarrelling over a mountain of beans. Thankfully there is an alternative – buying pre-shelled, frozen ones which, although inferior, do make a reasonable substitute. Serves 4.

25 minutes

1 bunch spring onions, finely chopped
1 tablespoon mint, chopped
juice of 1 lemon
2 tablespoons good virgin olive oil
salt & freshly ground black pepper
750 g / 1½ lb young broad beans, shelled

for the sauce
300 g / 12 oz Greek style yogurt
juice & grated zest of ½ lemon
2-3 tablespoons good fruity olive oil
1 fat clove of garlic, peeled & mashed
2 tablespoons mint or a combination of mint &
*   parsley, chopped*
salt & freshly ground black pepper

for the decoration
1 small purple or white onion, thinly sliced
a few sprigs mint

10

1

1   Fill a large pot of water and set over high heat to boil.

5

2   In a large mixing bowl, combine the spring onion together with the mint, lemon juice, olive oil and seasoning. Mix the dressing well.

3-5

3   When the water boils, plunge in the beans, blanch for about 2 minutes and strain. Immediately rinse the beans in cold water. Add the beans to the dressing and mix well.

4   To make the sauce, place the yogurt in a small mixing bowl. Add the other ingredients and mix well. To serve, pile a small mound of beans on individual plates and decorate with the sliced onion and a generous dollop of yogurt. Top with a sprig of mint.

3-5

FRIED ARTICHOKES SERVED WITH LEMON & GARLIC SAUCE

Artichokes come in many shapes, sizes and colours. The most suitable for this dish are the 'baby' French or American ones, which are available for only a short season. It is well worth looking out for them. Otherwise, use only the hearts of peeled large artichokes. To save the bother and time that peeling involves, use tinned or frozen artichoke hearts – some varieties are quite good. The hearts should be drained or defrosted and dried thoroughly before use. Serves 4.

30 minutes

3 eggs (size 3)
2 tablespoons water
salt & freshly ground black pepper
175 g/6 oz ground almonds
juice of 1 lemon
6 large, young artichokes
olive or peanut oil, for frying
Lemon & Garlic Sauce, to serve (see page 262)

5

5

1   In a wide, flat plate beat the eggs with the water, salt and pepper. Spread the ground almonds out on a tray or a wide, flat plate. Fill a large bowl with cold water and add the lemon juice.

2   Using a sharp knife, remove all the artichoke leaves, exposing the solid heart.
Remove the stems, if too tough and stringy, otherwise peel and trim.
Quarter the peeled artichokes and scrape out the hairy choke.
Immediately turn the artichokes in the acidulated water to prevent them discolouring.

10

3   If 'baby' artichokes are used, just remove the first layer of outer leaves, trim and peel the stem, halve, and immediately turn in lemon juice.
Allow 2–3 artichokes per person.

5

4   Heat the oil in a heavy-based frying pan.
Dip each artichoke quarter into the egg, then coat with ground almonds and fry over a moderate heat for about 5–8 minutes until golden-brown.
Serve hot with Lemon and Garlic Sauce.

10

FENNEL & GOAT'S CHEESE APPETIZER

Fennel is one of the most delicious salad vegetables. It has a clean, fresh, aniseed flavour and a crisp, juicy texture. The best way to serve fennel is raw, thinly sliced and flavoured with a few paper-thin onion rings and dressed in an olive oil vinaigrette or just with lemon juice and salt. Fennel also makes an interesting addition to crudités.

Goat's cheese logs are now available in many supermarkets. Select a semi-matured, rinded goat's cheese. When slicing the cheese use either a wire slicer or a sharp knife which has been dipped in boiling water. Serves 4.

30 minutes

6 medium bulbs of fennel
6 tablespoons good olive oil
350 g/12 oz goat's cheese log, cut into 12 round slices
freshly ground black pepper
1 teaspoon fennel seeds
1 teaspoon nigella seeds

5

10-15

1 Trim the fennel bulbs, discarding the tough outer layer and reserving some of the green fronds for garnish. Halve the fennel bulbs lengthways. Steam the fennel halves over a high heat for 8–10 minutes.

2 Meanwhile, heat the grill. Transfer the steamed fennel to the grill rack and brush generously with olive oil. Place a slice of cheese on each fennel half and sprinkle with the remaining oil, black pepper and the mixed seeds. Grill until the cheese bubbles and starts to brown. Serve either hot or at room temperature.

5-10

NAVATU EGGS

30 minutes

This recipe is based on one found in a charming book, *Gibraltar's Favourite Recipes,* published by the Gibraltar League of Hospital Friends. It is wonderfully simple and absolutely delicious. Serve with a simple salad as a first course or light lunch. Serves 4.

5

6 medium beef tomatoes
3 tablespoons olive oil
2 tablespoons chopped parsley
salt & freshly ground black pepper
100 g/4 oz raw, dry cured ham such as Prosciutto, jambon de Bayonne
6 large eggs
½ quantity of spicy tomato sauce (see page 269)
rocket leaves to decorate

1

1 Pre-heat the oven to 180°C/350°F/Gas Mark 4.

5

2 Remove the top of the tomatoes and set aside. Scoop out the flesh, being careful not to damage the skins.

3

3 Sprinkle the insides of the tomatoes with half the oil and dust with salt and pepper. Stuff them with half the chopped parsley and with the chopped ham.

15

4 Place the tomatoes in a well-greased baking tin and carefully break an egg into each. Sprinkle with the rest of the oil and parsley and bake in a medium oven until the eggs are softly set. Serve on a pool of cold spicy tomato sauce, surrounded by a few rocket leaves.

LEEK KUFTADAS

25 minutes

The leek is one of the most ancient of cultivated vegetables. It is mentioned in early Egyptian writing and was one of the ingredients mentioned in the Bible as being missed by the Jews after they left Egypt.

The recipe below is based on a Sephardi Jewish dish, which is traditionally served on the Passover – a holiday associated with the exodus from Egypt. Serves 4.

4

750 g/1½ lb leeks, washed & trimmed, with some of the green left on
150 g/6 oz feta cheese, coarsely grated or crumbed
3 eggs, beaten
50 g/2 oz – 75 g/3 oz matzo meal or bread crumbs
oil for frying

6

1 Slice the leeks into thin slices and steam them for 3-4 minutes. Rinse under cold water to cool and drain well.

5

2 Mix the leeks with the feta, eggs and matzo meal. If the mixture is too loose add a bit more matzo meal or breadcrumbs. Shape tablespoons of the mixture into flat patties.

10

3 Heat the oil in a large frying pan and fry the patties for 4-5 minutes on each side or until they are golden brown. Serve warm with Salsa Verde sauce (see page 265).

FRIED HALOUMI SERVED WITH FRUIT SAUCE

Haloumi belongs to a large family of cooking cheeses which also include Italian mozzarella and provolone. They are made from curds which have been cooked to give them their characteristic elastic, almost rubbery, texture. In Greece haloumi has been used since antiquity and was originally made from ewe's or goat's milk curds, though today cow's milk is also used. The curd is heated, drained and pressed. It is then cured in a mixture of herbs and salted water (originally sea water was used).

Haloumi may be eaten uncooked only when very fresh but the cheese really comes to life when it is cooked. Good haloumi does not lose its shape when heated and can therefore be grilled or fried, producing a steaky, meat-like texture.

This cheese is available in all Greek and Cypriot shops. Buy the kind which is kept in its brine and is not hard to the touch. Some pre-packed haloumi, which has recently begun to appear in many supermarkets, is quite good but shopping for it is a hit-and-miss affair. Remember to taste the haloumi before cooking; if too salty, soak in cold water for a few hours, changing the water frequently. Serves 4.

20 minutes

2 eggs (size 3)
2 tablespoons water
freshly ground black pepper
150 g/5 oz sesame seeds or ground hazelnuts
1 tablespoon finely chopped fresh thyme
1 teaspoon grated lemon rind
olive oil, for frying
75 g/3 oz haloumi per serving
sprigs of fresh mint, to garnish
½ quantity Raspberry Sauce (see page 273), to serve

5

5

1 Beat the eggs and the water in a large plate. Season with pepper. In another plate mix the sesame seeds or hazelnuts, thyme and lemon rind.

2 Heat some oil in a large, heavy-based frying pan. First dip each slice of cheese in the egg, then the sesame or hazelnut mixture. Place in the hot oil, reduce the heat and fry gently for about 4–5 minutes on each side or until the cheese slices are evenly golden.

8-10

1

3 Garnish with a sprig of mint and serve in a pool of tartish, cool fruit sauce.

HERB OMELETTE

Nothing can be simpler, quicker or more refreshing than this omelette. In the eastern Mediterranean appetisingly brilliant green and yellow omelettes are stuffed into pitta bread and sold for you to eat on the streets. When, in the beginning of the summer, fresh green onions are available use those, and use the green leaves too, unless they are shrivelled. Serves 4.

30 minutes

1 large bunch of spring onions or 1 large onion
1 bunch flat-leaf parsley
½ bunch of fresh coriander
6 eggs, beaten with 5 tablespoons water or milk
2 green chillies de-seeded & finely sliced (optional); see below
½ teaspoon ground coriander
½ teaspoon cumin seed
salt & freshly ground pepper
4 tablespoons olive or peanut oil

5

1

1 Heat the grill to maximum.

3

2 Put the onion and washed herbs into a food processor and process, starting and stopping the machine, until chopped but not puréed. Mix in the eggs, sliced chillies, flavouring and salt and pepper.

3 Heat the oil in a heavy-based frying pan and pour in the mixture. Allow it to coagulate for a minute and then, like making an omelette, draw the edges into the centre. Reduce the heat to minimum, cover and cook gently for about 5-8 minutes. Uncover and place the frying pan under the heated grill and cook for 5-6 minutes or until the omelette is puffy and has started to brown. Serve very hot or at room temperature.

15-20

NOTE: When de-seeding chillies it is important to remember that the seeds are the hottest part of the chilli and can cause real damage to sensitive skin, eyes and nose. Either wear gloves or wash your hands thoroughly after dealing with the chillies.

LAMB'S LIVER WITH LEMON & GARLIC

This belongs to a vast range of Turkish and Greek mezé dishes: tender pieces of lamb's liver, pink and juicy, flavoured with lemon, garlic and herbs. Serve it on a toasted pitta or bread so the delicious juices soak in.

Be careful not to overcook the liver because it will become dry and tough. It should be pink in the centre. If lamb's liver is not available use calf's liver. Serves 4.

15 minutes

1 tablespoon sweet paprika
3-4 tablespoons plain flour
500 g/1 lb lamb's liver, de-veined & cut into small pieces
4 tablespoons olive oil
3-4 sprigs of fresh thyme or 1 teaspoon dried thyme

1 small onion, peeled & sliced into thin rings
2 cloves of garlic, peeled & finely chopped
juice of 1 large lemon
salt & freshly ground black pepper
1-2 tablespoons chopped flat-leaf parsley
lemon wedges to decorate

3

1 Mix the paprika together with the flour and dip the liver in the mixture. The easiest way to do it is to put the seasoned flour into a large plastic bag, add the liver and shake well. Discard any loose flour.

1

2 Heat 3 tablespoons of the oil in a heavy-based frying pan. Add the thyme, onion and garlic and fry for a few seconds.

5-6

3 Add the seasoned liver and fry for 3-4 minutes, stirring all the time, until the liver is nicely browned. Add the lemon juice and continue frying for about 1 minute.

1

4 Remove from the heat, sprinkle with the rest of the olive oil, salt, pepper and the parsley. Decorate with lemon wedges and serve either hot or at room temperature.

SMOKED VEGETABLES SERVED WITH GREEN TAHINA SAUCE

This dish is based on the ancient Chinese technique of tea-smoking. The hot smoke partially cooks the vegetable, adding an irresistible smoky flavour. The list of vegetables below is arbitrary; any or all can be changed according to season and taste. Quail's eggs, tofu or hard goat's cheese can also be included. Star anise, which gives an interesting flavour, is obtainable from many supermarkets and all oriental shops.

This dish is easy and quick to make and, served with Green Tahina Sauce, it is a pleasant change from the traditional crudités.

One word of warning: the smoking process can ruin a saucepan. Use a covered wok or an old saucepan or flameproof casserole. Serves 4.

30 minutes

3 tablespoons fragrant tea, such as Lapsang Souchong
a few sprigs of fresh rosemary
a few sprigs of fresh thyme
3 strips of lemon zest
1 strip of orange zest
5–6 star anise
6 baby courgettes
6 baby carrots
6 baby sweetcorn
6 baby leeks
6 cherry tomatoes
6 cloves of garlic, peeled
3 tablespoons olive oil

10

Green Tahina Sauce (see page 258), to serve

15-20

1 Line an old saucepan, wok or flameproof casserole with a large piece of kitchen foil and place the tea, herbs, citrus zest and star anise on top. Cut another piece of foil large enough to fit the pan and place it on top of the smoking materials. Wash, dry and brush the vegetables with oil. Lay over the foil, cover the pan tightly and cook/smoke over a high heat for 10–15 minutes.

1

2 Serve the warm smoked vegetables in a pool of the bright green tahina sauce.

SPRING ONION & TOMATO EGGAH

The term eggah was coined by Claudia Roden and describes a mixture of eggs and various fillings which, when cooked, resemble a crustless quiche. Sliced into small squares, eggah can be served as a light lunch.

The fillings can vary to include cooked vegetables, chicken, meat or liver, pasta, spicy sausage and fish. The following version is an adaptation of a classic recipe. The final grilling of the eggah produces, if served immediately, a wonderful soufflé-like texture.

When making eggah or an omelette do not add the salt to the raw egg mixture as it tends to harden the eggs, making them rubbery; rather sprinkle the cooked dish with salt just before serving. Serves 4.

25 minutes

3 tablespoons good olive oil
2 bunches spring onions, trimmed & roughly chopped
4 medium tomatoes, peeled, de-seeded & roughly chopped
6 eggs, well beaten
100 g / 4 oz Katckaval, Caciocavallo or Pecorino cheese, coarsely grated or cubed
3 tablespoons dill or parsley, chopped
salt & freshly ground black pepper
lemon wedges

5

1

1 Pre-heat the grill to maximum.

10

2 Heat the oil in a heavy-based frying pan. Add the spring onions and fry for a minute or two until the onion starts to become transparent. Add the tomatoes, reduce the heat and cook, stirring frequently, for 5 minutes.

3 To the eggs, add the cheese, herbs, and pepper and mix well. Pour the mixture into the frying pan. As the mixture starts to set, draw the set bits into the centre, as you would for an omelette. Go on frying for 5-6 minutes or until the bottom starts to set. Remove from the heat and place under the hot grill. Grill for 5 minutes or until the top is set, fluffy and nicely browned. Either serve immediately or allow to cool to room temperature.

13-15

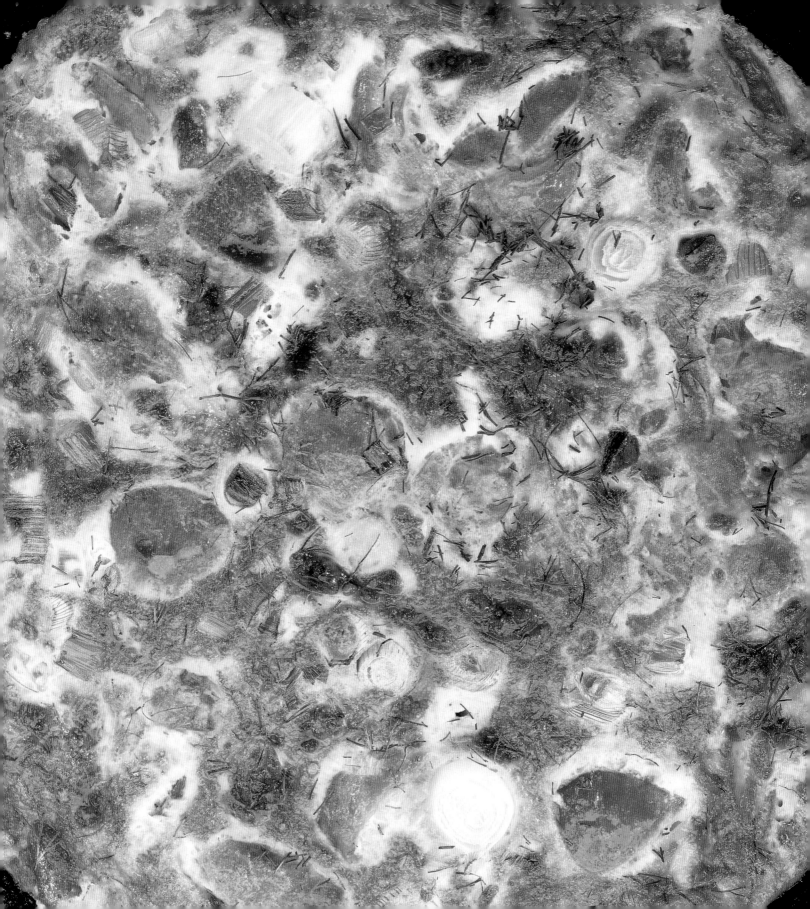

POLENTA 'PIZZAS'

Polenta is one of the most glorious Italian staples, but when the only cooking facilities were an open hearth and an iron tripod, making it used to be a real chore. Now, however, with better milling, better-quality corn and steadier heat, it takes less than 30 minutes (see page 215). These pizzas, made smaller, are delicious served as canapés. Serves 4.

25-30 minutes

100 g/4 oz sun-dried tomatoes in oil
12 x 75 mm/3 in cut rounds of cooked polenta (see page 215)
*   or 12 x 2 cm/³/4 in slices of polenta 'sausage'*
olive oil, for brushing
100 g/4 oz good mozzarella cheese, sliced
3 medium tomatoes, sliced into rings
1 clove of garlic, cut into thin slivers
1 tablespoon capers (optional)
75 g/3 oz Parmesan cheese, shaved into large flakes or grated

5

1

1 Heat the oven to 230°C/450°F/Gas Mark 8.

2

2 Put the sun-dried tomatoes and some of their oil into a food processor and process at high speed until puréed.

3 Brush the polenta slices generously with olive oil and arrange on a metal rack placed on a baking tray. Spread with the puréed sun-dried tomatoes and then lay on the mozzarella followed by the tomatoes, garlic slivers, capers, if used, and finally the Parmesan. Sprinkle with olive oil and bake in the pre-heated oven for

20

12–15 minutes. Serve the 'pizzas' hot, on a bed of shredded lettuce, each topped with a basil leaf.

PERFUMED TOFU

Tofu, or bean curd, by itself is a very tasteless affair indeed. Yet its characteristic blandness makes it ideal as a carrier of flavours. As with many basic ingredients, there are hundreds of ways to use tofu. You can marinate it in a strong, spicy sauce and then barbecue it. You can fry it, stuff it or cook it in a stew or curry. Below is a delicate and fragrant dish which will appeal even to those who don't like the idea of tofu.

Tofu is now available in most supermarkets, health shops and oriental stores. Try to purchase it in well-stocked oriental stores where it is sold very fresh, in its own liquid. In this state the tofu is delicate, mild and soft. When old, tofu tends to become rubbery and is not suitable for this dish. **Serves 4.**

40 minutes

peanut oil, for brushing
2 x 2.5cm / 1in slices of French bread per serving
1 teaspoon Chinese sesame oil, for brushing
1 medium onion, thinly sliced into rings
1 medium carrot, peeled & sliced into fine julienne strips
1 red pepper, de-seeded & sliced into fine julienne strips
2 fat cloves of garlic, thinly sliced
500 g / 1 lb 2 oz tofu, divided into 6 portions
6 small sprigs of fresh thyme
6 x 2.5cm / 1in sticks of lemon grass
6 cardamom pods, broken
3 tablespoons soy sauce

10

2 tablespoons Chinese sesame oil

1

1 Heat the oven to 190°C/375°F/Gas Mark 5.

2 Brush a large baking tin with the peanut oil and arrange the bread slices in it. Sprinkle each slice with about 1 teaspoon Chinese sesame oil. Put the tray at the bottom of the pre-heated oven and bake for 10–12 minutes or until the bread is browned and crisp.

10-12

3 Cut out 6 x 25 cm/10 in square pieces of kitchen foil. Brush the centre of each square generously with peanut oil. Place the onion, carrot, pepper and garlic at the centre of each square and lay the tofu on top. Top with the thyme, lemon grass and cardamom. Sprinkle with soy sauce and sesame oil. Seal the parcel by crimping the edges together.

10

4 Place on a baking tray and bake in the pre-heated oven for 10–12 minutes. Transfer the parcels on to individual plates, and place the bread in front. Allow each diner to tear the parcel so the delicious juices can soak into the crisp bread.

10

COS LETTUCE, TUNA, QUAIL'S EGGS & ROASTED PLUM TOMATOES

The cooking of the tuna for this salad can be done in advance, and if you always found tinned tuna dry and tasteless maybe cooking the fish in this way will make you think again! Serves 4 people as a starter or 2 people as a main course.

30 minutes

4 x 100 g/4 oz tuna steaks
3 cloves of garlic, chopped
1 sprig of fresh rosemary
1 stick of lemon grass, split in two
1 small red chilli, de-seeded & chopped (optional)
300 ml/10 fl.oz olive oil
12 quail's eggs
4 firm plum tomatoes, halved
3 tablespoons extra-virgin olive oil
salt & freshly ground black pepper
3 tablespoons mayonnaise
1 tablespoon balsamic vinegar
juice of 1 lemon
1 tablespoon finely chopped flat-leaf parsley
1 small head of cos lettuce, washed, drained & cut into strips
3 spring onions, thinly sliced
2 lemons, halved, to serve

12

1   First cook the tuna. Place the steaks in a heavy-based frying pan with the garlic, rosemary, lemon grass and chilli, if used, and pour over the olive oil. Bring to simmering point over a low heat and cook for about 10 minutes. Remove from the heat and leave to cool in the oil.

5

2   Meanwhile, cook the quail's eggs. Place them in a pan of cold water, bring to the boil and cook for 1 minute, then drain immediately. Peel the eggs under cold running water, cut in half and set aside.

5-8

3   Place the tomatoes in a roasting pan, sprinkle with 1 tablespoon of the extra-virgin olive oil, salt and pepper and bake in a pre-heated oven at 230°C/450°F/Gas Mark 8 for 5–8 minutes. Remove from the oven and keep warm..

3

4   Make the dressing: mix the mayonnaise, vinegar, the remaining extra-virgin olive oil, lemon juice and parsley together in a bowl. Whisk well with a fork and season.

2

5   Toss the cos lettuce, spring onions and quail's eggs in the dressing. Add the roasted plum tomatoes and crumble the warm tuna over the top. Serve with lemon halves, accompanied by warm pitta bread.

Cos Lettuce, Tuna, Quail's Eggs
& Roasted Plum Tomatoes,
and Lamb's Lettuce, Marinated Artichokes
& Parma Ham Salad with Parmesan Shavings
(page 89)

TUNA EGGAH

This recipe does not strictly fit the fresh idea of the book as the tuna used is tinned, but the dish is delicious and tuna is such an essential Mediterranean ingredient. Look around for white meat tuna preserved in either oil or brine which has started to appear on many supermarket shelves. If unobtainable ordinary tinned tuna will do. Unless you are on a diet, use tuna tinned in oil which should be drained thoroughly before use. Serve the eggah on a bed of salad either as a first course or as a main dish in a light lunch or supper. Serves 4.

30 minutes

3 tablespoons olive oil
1 large onion, peeled & coarsely chopped
2 cloves of garlic, peeled & coarsely chopped
2 tins of light meat tuna, well drained & flaked
1 50g/2oz tin of anchovies, drained & chopped
1 tablespoons capers, drained (optional)
6 eggs
3 tablespoons Greek style yogurt
freshly ground black pepper
3 teaspoons chopped dill or parsley
2 medium tomatoes, sliced into rings
lemon wedges for decoration

5

1

1   Pre-heat the grill to maximum.

5

2   Heat the oil in a heavy-based frying pan. Add the onion and garlic and fry for a few minutes until the onion starts to change colour. Add the tuna, anchovy and capers and continue frying for a minute or two.

8-10

3   Beat the eggs together with the yogurt, seasoning and herbs and pour over the frying mixture. Reduce the heat and, when the edges are starting to set, draw them with the help of a fork toward the centre – like making an omelette. Continue to fry for 2–3 minutes until almost set.

5-6

4   Place the sliced tomato on top of the setting mixture. Transfer the pan under the grill for about 5 minutes or until set and nicely browned. Serve decorated with lemon wedges. If more salt is needed sprinkle with a bit of coarse sea salt.

TARAMASALATA

Please do try to make taramasalata at home. It is easy to make and the results are very different from the pink, over-smooth concoction bought ready made. Originally this delicacy was made from the dried roes of grey mullet. These can be bought for a small fortune at many Greek and Turkish shops and they have a strong gamey flavour which, although deliciously savoury, is very much an acquired taste.

A special tarama paste is also available, which is much cheaper but I find it very salty. Instead I sometimes use smoked cod roe which is readily available at many fishmongers, with very good results. To remove excess saltiness, soak the roes in cold water or milk for a few hours.

Taramasalata is served either as a dip or together with pitta as a light first course. Or, try it, diluted with a bit of yogurt, as an original sauce with grilled fish or plainly boiled vegetables such as leeks, beans or even asparagus. Serves 4.

15 minutes

150 g/6 oz smoked cod roes, all membranes removed
100 g/4 oz crustless white bread, soaked in water & squeezed dry
1 small onion, finely grated
juice of 1 or more lemons (to taste)
grated zest of ½ lemon
150 ml/5 fl.oz extra virgin olive oil or a mixture of olive oil & ground nut oil

5

2-3

1 Put the cod roe, bread, onion, and lemon juice and zest into a food processor and process into a smooth paste.

5

2 With the machine still running, add the oil in a thin, steady stream and process until a thick cream is achieved. For sauce add either yogurt or cream until a consistency of pouring cream is achieved.

WARM MUSSEL SALAD

Although not traditional the following recipe is purely Mediterranean. It was first thought of as a starter for Christmas dinner and was a great success with everyone. It is elegant, light and full of flavour. Serves 4.

50 minutes

100 ml/4 fl.oz dry white wine
2 strips orange zest
1 strip grapefruit zest
2 bay leaves
1 teaspoon peppercorns
500 g/1 lb mussels, scrubbed & washed
1 large pink grapefruit
2 large oranges
1 small onion, sliced into thin rings

for the dressing
cooking liquid from the mussels
orange & grapefruit juice (see method)
1-2 teaspoon good honey
3 tablespoons hazelnut oil
salt & freshly ground pepper
3 tablespoons chopped dill

5-10

1 Place the wine and zests, together with the bay and peppercorns, in a large pan. Bring to the boil, add the mussels and reduce the heat to minimum. Cover and steam for about 5 minutes or until all the mussels are opened and cooked. Lift out the mussels and keep warm. Strain the liquid, and save it for the dressing. Discard any mussels that do not open fully.

6-8

2 To segment the grapefruit and oranges, cut a slice from both top and bottom to expose the flesh. Lay the fruit, cut side down, on a chopping board and then, using a serrated knife, slice away the peel exposing the flesh and removing all traces of the white pith. Hold the peeled fruit in the palm of your hand and, with a sharp knife, slice along the vertical membrane lines, leaving a perfectly peeled segment. When all segments are removed, squeeze the juice out of the flesh and reserve. Slice each segment to 2-3 pieces.

10

3 To make the dressing: place the cooking liquid, fruit juice, honey and oil in a small pan. Bring to the boil, skim, and keep boiling rapidly for 3-4 minutes until glossy and slightly thickened. Season with salt and pepper.

5

4 In a large salad bowl, mix the mussels with the fruit segments and onions. Pour the boiling sauce over the salad and mix well. Sprinkle the chopped dill and serve with chilled wine and chunky bread.

5

SALADS

SAVOURY EXOTIC FRUIT SALAD

25 minutes

Savoury fruit salad might sound a bit eccentric but this sweetish, refreshing salad is delicious served as an accompaniment to a spicy curry or can be served on a bed of lettuce as a light first course. Serves 4.

1 large mango
1 large pawpaw
1 fragrant melon such as Galia, or 1 pineapple
150 ml/5 fl.oz Greek yogurt
1 large white or red onion
2 tablespoons chopped fresh mint
1 tablespoons chopped fresh tarragon (optional)
juice & grated rind of 1 lime
¼ teaspoon each of ground ginger, ground cloves, ground fenugreek
*   & ground cardamom or 2 teaspoons good commercial curry powder*
½ teaspoon ground turmeric
salt
a few raspberries or wild strawberries, to decorate

5

a few sprigs of dill, to garnish

5

1 Peel the mango, remove the stone and slice the flesh to 2.5 cm/1 in cubes.

2 Halve the pawpaw, remove the seeds and, using a melon baller, shape the flesh into neat balls. Keep some of the pawpaw seeds for decoration; they are edible and have a surprisingly pleasant mustardy flavour.

5

3 Peel and cube the melon or pineapple and combine all the sliced fruit in a large serving bowl.

5

4 Mix the yogurt with the remaining ingredients, pour over the fruit and mix well. Decorate with pawpaw seeds, berries and a few sprigs of dill.

5

COOKED CARROT SALAD

25 minutes

A North African classic, which is good both warm or at room temperature and can also be served as a light first course. Serves 4.

50 ml/2 fl.oz good olive oil
1 tablespoon ground coriander
2 teaspoons cumin seeds
2 generous tablespoons clear honey
750 g/1½ lb carrots, peeled & sliced into
*   1 cm/½ in rings*

juice of 1 lemon
salt
1 tablespoon harissa
2 tablespoons chopped fresh coriander,
*   flat-leaf parsley or chervil*

5

1 Heat the oil in a heavy-based pan. Add the coriander and cumin seeds and fry for a few seconds until they emit a pleasant aroma. Add the honey and carrots and continue frying over a high heat, stirring from time to time, until the carrots begin to brown.

5

2 Add the lemon juice and salt, reduce the heat, cover and simmer very gently for 10–15 minutes or until the carrots are just cooked and still crunchy and most of the liquid has evaporated. (Check from time to time and if too dry add a few tablespoons of water or stock.) Add the harissa and the chopped herbs, mix well and serve.

12-18

Savoury Exotic Fruit Salad

CHICK-PEA, SALT COD, ROASTED RED ONION & PARSLEY SALAD

You can find pre-soaked salt cod in some delicatessens, otherwise ask your fishmonger or make enquiries at the fish counter at the supermarket. Serves 4 people as a starter or 2 people as a main course.

25 minutes

4 small red onions
3–4 tablespoons extra-virgin olive oil
salt & freshly ground black pepper
300 ml/10 fl.oz milk
300 ml/10 fl.oz water
2 bay leaves
450 g/l lb salt cod, pre-soaked overnight
1½ tablespoons sherry vinegar
1 clove of garlic, finely chopped
1 teaspoon French mustard
1 tablespoon flat-leaf parsley

5
400 g/14 oz cooked chick-peas

1   Peel the onions and place them in a roasting pan with a little oil and seasoning. Bake in a pre-heated oven at 200°C/400°F/Gas Mark 6 for about 20 minutes. Remove from the oven and leave to cool slightly, then cut into segments.

25

2   While the onions are cooking, place the milk and water in a large saucepan with the bay leaves and bring to the boil. Add the well-drained salt cod and simmer for about 10–15 minutes, skimming the cooking liquor when necessary. Drain the salt cod well when cooked.

15

3   Meanwhile, make the dressing: mix together the oil, vinegar, garlic, mustard and half the parsley. Whisk well with a fork and season with plenty of freshly ground black pepper. Toss the chick-peas, onion segments and warm cod in the dressing. Serve sprinkled with the remaining parsley. If served as a main course, accompany with roast or baked potatoes.

5

WARM SMOKED CHICKEN, RED ONION & SPINACH SALAD

You could also try this salad substituting the chicken with smoked quail, smoked mackerel or, even better, smoked eel. Serves 4 people as a starter or 2 people as a main course.

30 minutes

1 medium red onion, sliced
1 tablespoon soft brown sugar
3 tablespoons balsamic vinegar
3 tablespoons red wine vinegar
salt & freshly ground black pepper
1 teaspoon French mustard
2 tablespoons extra-virgin olive oil

3 tablespoons olive oil
300 g/10 oz baby spinach leaves, washed & well drained
600 g/1¼ lb smoked chicken, boned & roughly chopped
1 punnet of mustard & cress

5

1   First marinate the onion. In a bowl mix together the sugar, 1 tablespoon of the balsamic vinegar, the wine vinegar and a pinch of salt. Stir until the salt and sugar have dissolved, then add the onion. Toss well and leave to marinate for at least 20 minutes.

22

2   Make the dressing: mix together the mustard and the remaining balsamic vinegar in a bowl until well blended, then add the oils, whisking thoroughly with a fork or whisk. Season.

1-2

3   Dress the spinach with a couple of tablespoons of the dressing and toss well.

1

4   Place the chicken, the drained marinated onion and the remaining dressing in a frying pan and heat gently over a low flame, stirring frequently. When the dressing starts to simmer, remove from the heat. Spoon out on to the dressed spinach, sprinkle with the cress and serve. Boiled new potatoes would be a perfect accompaniment.

1

FENNEL, PEAR, PECAN NUT & DOLCELATTE SALAD

Dolcelatte is a deliciously mild creamy blue cheese produced in northern Italy. If you prefer a stronger cheese use Gorgonzola or a mature stilton. Serves 4 people as a starter or 2 people as a main course.

20 minutes

50 g/2 oz pecan nuts, roughly chopped
2 medium bulbs of fennel, thinly sliced
juice of ½ lemon
30 g/1 oz fresh ginger, peeled & cut into very fine strips or grated
1 tablespoon balsamic vinegar

3 tablespoons extra-virgin olive oil
salt & freshly ground black pepper
1 comice pear, ripe but firm, washed
225 g/8 oz dolcelatte cheese, cut into small chunks
1 tablespoon finely chopped chives

5

1   Toast the pecan nuts in a pre-heated oven at 220°C/425°F/Gas Mark 7 for about 8–10 minutes until slightly darkened. Remove from the oven and leave to cool.

10-15

2   Toss the fennel with the lemon juice to prevent discoloration.

1

3   Make the dressing: mix the ginger, vinegar and oil in a bowl. Whisk with a fork and season.

1

4   Slice the pear and toss with the fennel, half the nuts and the dressing. Sprinkle with the dolcelatte, the remaining nuts, the chives and freshly ground black pepper. Serve accompanied with crusty bread or toasted sun-dried tomato ciabatta bread.

3-4

PRAWN & ORANGE SALAD

The inspiration for this unusual combination comes from Morocco. There, the salad is made from a local variety of aromatic oranges which have a delightful, slightly bitter flavour. They are simply peeled, sliced and mixed with onion and a dressing of olive oil.

The salad below can be made with any good sharp oranges and makes a refreshing dish to serve either as a light lunch or as an elegant first course. Serves 4.

10 minutes

3 tablespoons virgin olive or walnut oil
juice of 1 small orange
1 teaspoon grated orange zest
salt & freshly ground black pepper
3 large oranges, peeled & sliced into thin rings
1 bunch of spring onions, trimmed & chopped
300 g/12 oz cooked peeled prawns

7

3 tablespoons dill

1

1   In a large salad bowl combine the oil with the orange juice, zest and the seasoning and mix well.

2-3

2   Add the rest of the ingredients and toss gently. Serve decorated with a few unpeeled prawns and sprigs of dill.

SALATA DE PIPINO (CUCUMBER SALAD)

This pale green and refreshing salad is ideal for serving with fish dishes. The best cucumbers to use are the small, sweet, hard, intensely green variety imported from the Mediterranean.

Traditionally this salad is flavoured with white pepper but, if you do not mind little black specks in your salad, use black pepper as it is more aromatic. Serves 4.

10 minutes

3 tablespoons white wine vinegar
2 tablespoons water
1 clove of garlic, mashed
salt & freshly ground black pepper
1-2 teaspoons sugar or honey (optional)
500 g/1 lb cucumber

4-5

2 tablespoons chopped dill or mint

1

1   Mix the dressing in a large salad bowl.

2   Slice the cucumber into paper thin rounds, add to the dressing together with the chopped herbs,

3-5

mix well and serve.

WARM SALAD OF SQUID & WATERCRESS WITH ROASTED PEANUT DRESSING

Look for blanched (skinless) unsalted peanuts in health shops or oriental grocers. Serves 4 people as a starter or 2 people as a main course.

25 minutes

100 g/4 oz unsalted peanuts
salt & freshly ground black pepper
2 tablespoons white wine vinegar
2 tablespoons ketjap manis (see page 48)
1½ tablespoons sake
1 tablespoon balsamic vinegar
½ tablespoon honey
4 tablespoons extra-virgin olive oil
½ small red onion, diced
450 g/l lb small squid (12.5–15 cm/5–6 in), cleaned & cut into rings
rind of 1 lemon
200 g/7 oz watercress, washed & drained
12 cherry tomatoes, halved

5-8

1 Toast the peanuts in a pre-heated oven at 230°C/450°F/Gas Mark 8 until evenly browned. Remove from the oven and leave to cool.

8-10

2 Bring a saucepan of salted water acidulated with the wine vinegar to the boil.

2

3 Meanwhile, make the dressing: in a bowl mix together the ketjap manis, sake, balsamic vinegar, honey, two-thirds of the extra-virgin olive oil and the onion. In a food processor coarsely grind the peanuts, then add to the dressing, mix well and season.

3

4 Drop the squid rings into the boiling water, return to the boil and immediately drain well. Toss the squid with the lemon rind and the remaining oil in a bowl.

3

5 To assemble the salad, mix the watercress and cherry tomatoes together, pile the warm squid on top and finally spoon on the peanut dressing.

5

WARM SALAD OF POTATO, ROCKET & SMOKED MACKEREL WITH A HORSERADISH & RED ONION DRESSING

30 minutes

Serves 4 people as a starter or 2 people as a main course.

450 g / 1 lb new potatoes, well-scrubbed & quartered
170 g / 6 oz creamed horseradish
½ small red onion, finely diced
3 tablespoons crème fraîche
juice of 1 lemon

3 tablespoons extra-virgin olive oil
1 tablespoon finely chopped flat-leaf parsley
salt & freshly ground black pepper
4 smoked mackerel fillets
100 g / 4 oz rocket leaves, washed & drained

3-5

15-20

1   Bring a saucepan of salted water to the boil, add the potatoes and simmer gently for 15–20 minutes until tender.

2   Meanwhile, make the dressing: mix together the horseradish, onion, crème fraîche, lemon juice, oil and parsley in a bowl. Whisk well with a fork, season and set aside.

1

3   Warm the mackerel fillets under the grill or in a pre-heated oven at 230°C/450°F/Gas Mark 8 for about 5 minutes, then flake roughly.

8

4   When the potatoes are cooked, drain well and toss in a bowl with the mackerel and the dressing. Arrange on a bed of rocket leaves and serve sprinkled with freshly ground black pepper.

3

LAMB'S LETTUCE, MARINATED ARTICHOKES & PARMA HAM SALAD WITH PARMESAN SHAVINGS

10 minutes

Marinated artichokes are readily available in good delicatessens and most supermarkets, but if you want to make your own there are instructions given in the note below. Serves 4 people as a starter or 2 people as a main course.

1 tablespoon sherry vinegar
1½ tablespoons hazelnut oil
2 tablespoons extra-virgin olive oil
salt & freshly ground black pepper
225 g / 8 oz lamb's lettuce, washed & drained

8 thin slices of Parma ham, cut into strips
4 marinated artichokes, cut into segments
2 plum tomatoes, cut into segments
100 g / 4 oz Parmesan cheese

5

1-2

1   Make the dressing: mix the vinegar and oils together in a bowl. Whisk well with a fork, and season.

2   Assemble on a serving plate the lamb's lettuce, Parma ham, artichokes and tomatoes. Sprinkle with the dressing. Using a potato peeler, shave the Parmesan directly on to the salad.

3-4

NOTE: To make your own marinated artichokes, take small firm fresh globe artichokes, peel back the outer leaves until you almost reach the core, trim the base and peel away the fibrous skin of the stalks. Cook in boiling salted water acidulated with lemon juice or white wine vinegar for 20–40 minutes or until a knife can easily pierce the base. Drain well and leave to cool. Remove the choke, then pack tightly into a jar with garlic, bay leaves, peppercorns and chilli. Cover with extra-virgin olive oil and seal. Keep in a cool dry place or in the fridge.

BROCCOLI, CAULIFLOWER & ROASTED PEPPER SALAD
WITH ANCHOVY DRESSING

Anchovies are widely used in the Italian cooking repertoire both as an ingredient and a flavouring. Their preparation and preservation hasn't changed much since the days Roman matrons and fishmongers began layering the fresh fish with rock salt in small barrels. Serves 4 people as a starter or 2 people as a main course.

25 minutes

2 small yellow peppers
2 small red peppers
salt & freshly ground black pepper
225 g/8 oz broccoli florets
225 g/8 oz cauliflower florets
4 anchovy fillets in oil
2 tablespoons balsamic vinegar
juice of 1 lemon
1 teaspoon English mustard
5 tablespoons olive oil
1 clove of garlic, peeled
1 teaspoon clear honey
1 tablespoon chopped flat-leaf parsley

2

20

1 Roast the peppers in a pre-heated oven at 230°C/450°F/Gas Mark 8 for about 15–20 minutes, or until the skins have blistered. Remove from the oven, place in a bowl and cover with cling-film. Leave to cool slightly, then skin, de-seed and cut the flesh into strips.

7-8

2 While the peppers are roasting, bring a saucepan of salted water to the boil. Drop in the broccoli, return to the boil and cook for 1 minute. Remove the broccoli with a perforated spoon and rinse under cold running water. Repeat this process for the cauliflower but this time cook for 3–4 minutes.

3-4

3 Make the dressing: place the anchovies, vinegar, lemon juice, mustard, oil, garlic and honey in a liquidizer and whizz until well blended. Adjust the seasoning and add a little water if the dressing is too thick. Toss the vegetables together in the dressing and serve sprinkled with the parsley, accompanied by bruschetta.

NOTE: Bruschetta is toasted ciabatta bread rubbed with garlic and sprinkled with extra-virgin olive oil (see page 200).

COOKED BEANS & TOMATO SALAD

30 minutes

Cooked vegetable salads are eaten all around the Mediterranean. They can be served hot but are at their best at room temperature. Serves 4.

4 tablespoons strong olive oil
250 g/8 oz onion, coarsely chopped
5-8 fat cloves of garlic, peeled & coarsely chopped
1-2 green or red chillies, sliced (optional)
4 medium tomatoes, peeled, de-seeded & coarsely chopped
salt
500 g/1 lb fine French beans, topped & tailed

10 *chopped parsley & lemon wedges for decoration*

6-8

1 Heat the oil in a heavy-based frying pan. Add the onion, garlic and chillies and fry over high heat for about 4-5 minutes or until the garlic starts to brown.

5

2 Add the tomatoes and salt. Reduce the heat and simmer, stirring, for a few minutes.

10

3 Add the beans, mix well, cover the pan and steam for 8-10 minutes, stirring the mixture once or twice. The beans should remain crunchy. Serve in a warmed dish, decorated with lemon wedges and parsley.

CELERY & TOMATO SALAD

12-15 minutes

This salad is colourful, easy to make and delicious as an accompaniment to a main course.

The best celery to use is the green leafy variety that is easily obtained from Greek and Indian grocers. Serves 4.

3 tablespoons olive oil
juice of 1 lemon
salt
1 large head of celery, trimmed and chopped
2 large beef tomatoes
100 g/4 oz black olives, chopped

10 *2 tablespoons chopped flat-leaf parsley*

1

1 In a large salad bowl mix the oil, lemon juice and salt.

1

2 Add the rest of the ingredients and mix well.

AUBERGINE & TOMATO SALAD

The aubergine is one of the essential ingredients of the Mediterranean kitchen. It is made into numerous salads, dips and pastes, stuffed, stewed and even made into a delicious sweet jam and into preserves.

The following recipe is a particularly healthy and unusual combination of cooked aubergine and fresh tomatoes. Serves 4.

30 minutes

4 tablespoons good olive oil
1 large onion, peeled & finely chopped
3 cloves of garlic, peeled & chopped
1 or more red chillies, de-seeded & sliced
a few strips of lemon zest
750 g / 1½ lb aubergine, trimmed and cubed
300 g / 12 oz tomatoes, grated on a coarse grater
salt & freshly ground black pepper
3 tablespoons parsley or mint, chopped
2 tablespoons olive oil

5-10

lemon wedges

5

1 Heat the first quantity of oil in a heavy-based frying pan, add the onion, garlic, chillies and lemon zest and fry, on high heat, for 3-4 minutes, stirring constantly.

20

2 In the meantime, put the cubed aubergine into the food processor and process, starting and stopping the machine until the mixture is finely chopped but not puréed. Add the aubergine to the pan, reduce the heat, cover and simmer for about 15 minutes.

15

3 Uncover and season. Increase the heat and cook for a few more minutes until most of the liquid has evaporated. Switch the heat off and remove the lemon zest. Add the tomatoes and herbs and mix well. Turn into a serving dish, sprinkle with the olive oil, decorate with lemon wedges and serve.

NOTE: When dealing with chillies it is important to remember that the seeds (the hottest part) can cause real damage to sensitive skin, to the eyes and nose. Either wear gloves to chop chillies or make sure you wash your hands thoroughly after handling them.

RAW BEETROOT & APPLE SALAD

You either love or hate beetroot. For many people it is delicious, especially raw. Young uncooked beets have a surprisingly sweet, earthy flavour and a pleasant crunchy texture.

If you like your beetroot cooked, bake it in a hot oven for about 1–1½ hours until just soft. Allow to cool slightly, then peel under cold water. (Or, of course, buy cooked beetroot.)

The best apples to use are any sweet–sour variety like Cox's, Granny Smith or russets, when in season. Use the apples unpeeled as the peel adds contrasting colour to the salad. Serves 4.

20 minutes

2 tablespoons cider vinegar
1 tablespoon ready-made English mustard or powder
salt & freshly ground black pepper
75 ml/3 fl.oz peanut oil
500 g/1 lb peeled, raw beetroot sliced into 1 cm/½ in cubes or grated coarsely
225 g/8 oz tart eating apples, cored & thinly sliced

10

2 tablespoons coarsely chopped fresh flat-leaf parsley or dill

5 1 Mix the vinegar with the mustard, salt and pepper. Add the oil gradually and whisk until amalgamated.

2 Put the beetroot and apple into a large mixing bowl. Pour over the dressing, sprinkle over the parsley or dill and
5 mix well. Serve either chilled or at room temperature.

NOTE: Cold pressed peanut oil, if available, is especially good with this salad. It can sometimes be purchased in speciality or health shops.

FENNEL & PINK GRAPEFRUIT SALAD

20 minutes **A refreshing and different summer salad. Serves 4.**

400 g/14 oz fennel, washed well
2 large pink grapefruits
6 tablespoons hazelnut oil
2 teaspoons fragrant clear honey
2 *salt & freshly ground black pepper*

1 Trim the fennel, discarding the outer leaves and stems if tough. Keep some of the green fronds to garnish. Slice
3-5 the bulbs crossways into very thin rings.

2 To segment the grapefruit, cut a slice off both top and bottom to expose the pink flesh. Lay the grapefruit, cut side up, on a chopping board and then, using a serrated knife, slice away the peel, exposing the flesh and removing all traces of the white pith. Hold the peeled grapefruit in the palm of your hand and, using a sharp knife, slice along the vertical membrane lines, leaving a perfectly peeled segment. When all the segments are
10 removed squeeze the juice out of the flesh, reserving 4 tablespoons. Drink the rest – it's good for you!

3 Combine the fennel and grapefruit in a large mixing bowl. Whisk the reserved grapefuit juice with the oil,
5 honey and salt and pepper to taste. Pour over the fennel and grapefruit, mix well and serve.

MOROCCAN LEMON SALAD

If you love lemon this is the salad for you. It is delightfully tart and goes very well with any fried or grilled fish especially with the oilier ones like sardines and mackerels. The relish improves with storing. It will keep in the refrigerator for up to two weeks.

You can peel the lemons if you don't like things too bitter, in which case include some grated zest to intensify the lemony flavour. Serves 2.

10 minutes

4 ripe, thin-skinned lemons
2 teaspoons olive oil
2 teaspoons or more harissa (see page 257)
1 bunch flat-leaf parsley, chopped

6

2-3   1   Slice the lemons into thin rounds, discarding any pips.

2-3   2   Add the rest of the ingredients and mix well.

ORANGE & OLIVE SALAD

An interesting salad of Moroccan origin. It is very easy to make and improves wwhen kept. Sealed in a jar and refrigerated, it will last for up to a week. Seville oranges, when in season, are best for the salad, but any tart orange will do.

Greek broken olives are obtainable from many Greek and Middle Eastern shops. They are sold in their marinating liquid, which includes coriander seeds, sliced lemon and garlic. Taste the olives before use – if they are too salty either rinse or soak them in cold water until the right amount of saltiness is reached.

This refreshing salad is best served together with bean stews or any other substantial main course. Serves 4.

15 minutes

4–5 oranges, peeled & cut into 3 mm / ⅛ in slices
100 g / 4 oz Greek broken green olives
2 teaspoons cumin seeds or 1 teaspoon ground cumin
1 tablespoon Moroccan harissa (optional)
50 ml / 2 fl.oz olive, peanut or sesame oil
salt
2 tablespoons chopped fresh dill
1 cos lettuce, outer leaves discarded, washed & dried, to serve

5

1 Put the sliced oranges and olives into a bowl. If using cumin seeds, roast them in a dry frying pan, until they begin to pop and emit a delicious, savoury aroma. Add to the oranges. Add the remaining ingredients and toss gently but thoroughly. Serve on a bed of cos lettuce leaves.

10

NOTE: Instead of Moroccan harissa you could add chopped fresh chillies or chilli powder to taste.

SPINACH IN SESAME DRESSING

15 minutes

The simplest and one of the most delicious ways of serving spinach. Serves 4.

500 g / 1 lb baby spinach leaves, washed well   *salt*
2 tablespoons sherry or rice vinegar   *75 g / 3 oz sesame seeds*
3 tablespoons Chinese sesame oil   *1 tablespoon pine-nuts, slightly browned in a little oil*
1 teaspoon clear honey   *1 small chilli, chopped (optional)*

5

1 Heat a steamer and steam the spinach, stirring from time to time, for about 4–5 minutes or until the leaves are wilted but still bright green. Chop the spinach coarsely and keep warm.

6-7

2 In a small saucepan mix the vinegar, oil, honey and salt to taste. Bring to the boil and pour over the spinach. Roast the sesame seeds in a dry frying pan until they start to pop and emit a pleasant roasted aroma. Add to the spinach and mix well. Sprinkle with pine-nuts and chilli, if used, and serve warm.

3

FRIED SPINACH SALAD

Spinach is one of the most popular vegetables around the Mediterranean. It appears in salads and stuffings, adds colour to pasta or gnocchi and is served to accompany meat or fish.

The word spinach is sometimes misleading as it is used as a collective term to describe green, edible leaves. The dish can also be made successfully from chard or beet leaves which have an intense, earthy flavour and are less muddy, therefore needing less preparation. Chard and beet are available almost all year round in many Indian, Greek and Turkish grocers. Serves 4.

25 minutes

1 kg/2 lb chard or spinach, washed well
2 medium onions, peeled & chopped
4 tablespoons good olive oil
salt & freshly ground pepper
a few scrapings of nutmeg
juice of 1 orange
grated zest of ½ orange
1 tablespoon olive oil
50 g/2 oz pine-nuts previously browned in a bit of oil
5 *lemon wedges*

5

1   Wash the spinach in a few changes of water, remove tough stems and wilted leaves and chop coarsely. If using chard – wash and trim the stems, lay a few leaves on top of each other, roll into a thick cigar shape and slice across thinly.

2   In a heavy-based frying pan heat half the first quantity of oil. Add half the onion and fry for a minute or two until the onion starts to become transparent. Add half of the spinach and fry, on high flame, for about 4–5 minutes until the leaves wilt and most of the liquid has evaporated. Lift into a serving dish. Repeat with the rest

10-12 of the spinach, the onion and the oil.

3   Add the seasoning, dress with orange juice, orange zest and olive oil and mix well. Decorate with the pine-nuts

2-3 and lemon wedges and serve either warm or at room temperature.

RAW ARTICHOKE SALAD

This attractive salad has a surprisingly fresh, earthy flavour and goes very well with cold or cured meats, poached egg or just bread and butter for a light and elegant supper dish. It comes from the North African coast of the Mediterranean, where artichokes are supposed to have healing powers. The water in which the artichokes are cooked is drunk to improve health and help with problems of potency and fertility.

To clean the artichokes, first peel all the leaves exposing the chokey heart. With a sharp teaspoon scrape away the choke. Trim, and remove the stem if too woody. Immediately plunge the peeled artichoke into cold acidulated water as the cut surface blackens very quickly. Do not throw away the leaves; use them to decorate the salad. Serves 4.

25 minutes

4 large artichokes, cleaned as above
1 bunch spring onions
2 large tomatoes, peeled, de-seeded & roughly chopped
3 tablespoons virgin olive oil
juice of 1 lemon or to taste
1 clove of garlic, finely chopped
½ lemon sliced into thin slices, each slice cut into small wedges
salt & freshly ground black pepper

5

3 tablespoons parsley, roughly chopped

15

1 Peel the artichokes as explained above.

2 Combine the rest of the ingredients in a large salad bowl and mix well. Slice the artichokes into thin crescents and immediately coat with the dressing. Decorate with artichoke leaves and serve. The salad improves if left to marinate for a few hours. The artichoke hearts will not discolour once they are coated in the dressing.

5

FRENCH BEAN, PRAWN & AVOCADO SALAD

25 minutes

Don't be tempted to skip the sesame seeds, and make sure you toast them lightly (just golden) in a pan or in the oven: they are the 'secret ingredient' of this recipe. Serves 4 people as a starter or 2 people as a main course.

10

2 tablespoons sesame seeds
450 g/1 lb French beans, topped, tailed & cut in half
juice & rind of 1 lemon
1 tablespoon balsamic vinegar
1 tablespoon ketjap manis (see page 158)
3 tablespoons extra-virgin olive oil

½ small chilli, de-seeded & finely chopped (optional)
salt & freshly ground black pepper
225 g/8 oz Norwegian prawns
4 spring onions, thinly sliced
2 avocados, stoned, peeled and cut into small chunks

2

1 Toast the sesame seeds in a heavy-based frying pan over a medium heat, tossing frequently until golden. Set aside to cool.

6

2 Bring a saucepan of salted water to a brisk boil. Drop in the French beans, return to the boil and cook for a couple of minutes until tender. Drain and refresh under cold running water.

2-3

3 Meanwhile make the dressing: mix together the lemon juice and rind, the vinegar, manis and oil in a bowl. Add the chilli, if used. Whisk well with a fork and season.

2-3

4 Toss the well-drained beans, the prawns, spring onions and the avocado in the dressing. Serve sprinkled with the sesame seeds.

WARM SALAD OF BABY CORN, COURGETTES & BEAN SPROUTS

15 minutes

Tofu, or bean curd, is made from puréed soy beans that have been cooked, curdled and then pressed into cakes, usually square. Tofu is pure protein, rich in minerals and vitamins but extremely low in fat and cholesterol. Serves 4 people as a starter or 2 people as a main course.

100 g/4 oz silken tofu
25 g/1 oz fresh ginger, peeled
4–5 stalks of coriander
1 clove of garlic, peeled
1 small Thai chilli, de-seeded (optional)
1 tablespoon balsamic vinegar
1 teaspoon clear honey
juice of 1 lemon
2 tablespoons ketjap manis (see page 158)

2 tablespoons olive oil
salt & freshly ground black pepper
1½ tablespoons sesame oil
200 g/7 oz baby sweetcorn, quartered
2 medium courgettes, cut into thin batons
1 medium red pepper, cut into thin strips
75 g/3 oz bean sprouts, rinsed & drained
1 head of radicchio, thinly sliced
4 spring onions, thinly sliced

10

1-2

1 Make the dressing: combine the tofu, ginger, coriander stalks, garlic, chilli, vinegar, honey, lemon juice, ketjap manis and oil in a liquidizer and whizz until smooth. Season and if too thick dilute with a little water. Set aside.

2-3

2 Heat the sesame oil in a wok or large frying pan and toss in it the baby sweetcorn, courgettes, red pepper and bean sprouts. Season and stir-fry for a couple of minutes.

2-3

3 Prepare a base of radicchio on a serving plate. Spoon on the stir-fried vegetables, then the dressing, and serve sprinkled with the spring onions.

BEAN & GINGER SALAD

This South Asian-inspired salad is excellent as part of a cold buffet or to accompany various main dishes.

You can use a wide variety of different coloured fresh beans and peas such as runner beans, French beans, yellow beans and mangetout or any other permutation. Baby sweetcorn and water chestnuts add variety and cool crunch to the spicy salad.

From time to time one can find fresh water chestnuts in specialist Asian shops. These little nuts look muddy and uninspiring and are definitely difficult to peel, but what a difference to the tinned variety in flavour and texture. It's well worth the trouble. Serves 4.

20 minutes

750 g / 1½ lb fresh beans & peas
5 cloves of garlic, peeled
5 shallots, peeled
5 cm / 2 in piece of fresh ginger, peeled
50 ml / 2 fl.oz sesame or peanut oil
1–2 chillies, thinly sliced (optional)
3 tablespoons dark soy sauce
3 tablespoons rice or cider vinegar
1 generous tablespoon clear honey
½ teaspoon salt
2 tablespoons Chinese sesame oil
100 g / 4 oz water chestnuts, sliced

5

1 Heat a steamer and steam the beans and peas over a high heat for 4–5 minutes.

3

2 Put the garlic, shallots and ginger into a food processor and process, starting and stopping the machine until minced but not mushy.

10

3 Heat the oil in a wok or heavy-based frying pan and add the garlic mixture and chillies, if used. Fry over a high heat for a few minutes, scraping and mixing well, until the mixture begins to take colour. Add the soy sauce, vinegar, honey, salt and sesame oil, bring to the boil and reduce over a high heat until the sauce is slightly thickened and glossy (about 3 minutes).

3

4 When the beans are ready, transfer them to a serving bowl, add the water chestnuts, pour the boiling sauce over and mix well. Serve either warm or at room temperature.

AHIVETCH OR GAIVETCH

This delicious cooked vegetable salad is probably of Turkish origin but appears, in many guises, all over the Mediterranean. Any seasonal vegetables are healthy and ideally suited to this piquant concoction. When grapes are plentiful I like to add some seedless green ones as they add a delightful sweetness. Serves 4.

25 minutes

3 tablespoons olive oil
1 large onion, peeled & chopped
3 cloves of garlic, peeled & chopped
3-4 celery stems, coarsely chopped
150 g/6 oz French beans, topped, tailed & sliced
2 courgettes, sliced into rings
1 red & 1 green pepper, de-seeded & sliced into strips
100 g/4 oz fresh peas
75 g/3 oz seedless grapes (optional)
2 large tomatoes, peeled, de-seeded & coarsely chopped
a few sprigs of fresh oregano, savory & tarragon or ½ teaspoons each of dried chopped parsley

5

3-4

1   Heat the oil in a heavy-based frying pan. Add the onion and garlic and fry for a few minutes or until the onion starts to take colour.

2   Add the vegetables and grapes, stir well and reduce the heat. Continue frying for about 10–15 minutes. Add the tomato and herbs, increase the heat and continue frying for a minute or two until the tomato is hot. Serve decorated with chopped parsley either warm or at room temperature.

17-20

PANZANELLA

One of the advantages of salad dishes is the opportunity to dunk bread into the wonderfully savoury juice that the vegetables produce. Panzanella is a way of enjoying the tasty combination of olive oil, lemon and tomato juices without dunking the bread.

This is a clever way of using stale bread and making a salad into a more substantial dish, ideal as a light summer lunch with a glass of chilled white wine.

Bread salads are eaten all around the Mediterranean and they differ in the types of bread used. Panzanella is made from stale Tuscan bread in Italy; in Greece and Turkey, pitta is used. Why not try making the salad from the soft, round pitta that has started to appear in many shops and supermarkets. Whatever bread you choose, make sure that it is a good quality, traditionally-baked loaf. Serves 4.

25 minutes

5 tablespoons good olive oil
juice of 1 large lemon, or more to taste
3 tablespoons water
salt & freshly ground black pepper
4 medium, ripe tomatoes, peeled & sliced
1 large purple onion, sliced
1 large red pepper, cored & sliced
4 round pittas or 6 slices of tasty, good white bread
1 large bunch of flat-leaf parsley, leaves only, chopped or
½ bunch of parsley & the same quantity basil

5-7

2-3

1 In a large salad bowl combine the oil, lemon juice, water and seasoning. Add the vegetables and toss well.

2 Tear the pitta or bread into small pieces and add to the salad, together with the chopped herbs and mix well. Allow the salad to stand for about 10 minutes for the bread to soak up the juices. Taste the salad and add more lemon and salt if necessary as bread tends to neutralise acidity.

15

SWEET POTATO & CHERRY SALAD

Originally this salad was made with cherries and the combination of these and sweet potatoes is wonderful when they are both in season.

The salad is open to many variations. The cherry season is short, so try it with different sour fruit. It works very well with blueberries, loganberries and even cranberries, especially rehydrated dried ones. In the pomegranate season use pomegranate seeds which give the salad a special bejewelled, festive look. Serves 4.

20 minutes

750 g/1½ lb orange fleshed sweet potato, unpeeled,
*   scrubbed & sliced into 4 cm/1½ in cubes*
1 medium red onion, sliced into thin rings
225 g/8 oz sour cherries, stoned
3 tablespoons whole fresh coriander leaves

For the dressing
1 scant tablespoon mustard powder
1 generous tablespoon good clear honey
75 ml/3 fl.oz raspberry or any other aromatic vinegar
75 ml/3 fl.oz olive or peanut oil
salt & freshly ground black pepper

5

1   First make the dressing. Put all the ingredients into a jar, close tightly and shake well until thoroughly amalgamated. Transfer the dressing to a large mixing bowl.

3

2   Steam the sweet potatoes until tender but not mushy (8–10 minutes). Immediately fold the steamed potato into the dressing. Add the onion rings, cherries and 2 tablespoons coriander leaves and fold in gently. Garnish with the remaining coriander and serve either warm or cold.

12-15

NOTE: After cutting, sweet potatoes tend to discolour very quickly. To prevent this, immerse immediately in cold, acidulated water (2 tablespoons vinegar or lemon juice to 575 ml/1 pint water).

Morello cherries are a bit *too* sour for this salad but any sour–sweet eating cherry will do. The fleshy American cherries can be used in emergencies.

CHICKEN, OYSTER MUSHROOM & FRISÉE SALAD
WITH PINE-NUTS & SULTANAS

30 minutes

Combining savoury flavours with sweet ones is a habit that goes back to Medieval times and the influence of the Moors in the Mediterranean, particularly in southern Spain and Italy. Serves 4 people as a starter or 2 people as a main course.

2 x 225 g/8 oz chicken breasts, skinned
600 ml/1 pint water
80 g/3 oz unsalted butter
juice of 1 lemon
salt & freshly ground black pepper
100 g/4 oz pine-nuts
350 g/12 oz oyster mushrooms, stalks removed
100 g/4 oz sultanas
1 teaspoon Dijon mustard
3 tablespoons extra-virgin olive oil
1½ tablespoons balsamic vinegar
1 small clove of garlic, finely chopped
1 tablespoon finely chopped chives
5
1 small head of frisée lettuce, washed & drained

20-25

1 First poach the chicken breasts. Bring the water to the boil in a saucepan and add one-third of the butter and half the lemon juice. Season, then add the chicken breasts and simmer for about 15 minutes. Turn off the heat and leave the chicken to cool in the cooking juices for 5–10 minutes, then remove and cut into strips.

5-10

2 Toast the pine-nuts on a baking tray in a pre-heated oven at 230°C/425°F/Gas Mark 8 for 5–10 minutes or until golden. Remove from the oven and leave to cool.

5-6

3 Melt the remaining butter in a frying pan and when it begins to sizzle, toss in the mushrooms and sultanas and season well. Remove from the heat and toss the mushrooms and sultanas with the chicken and pine-nuts in a bowl.

3-4

4 Make the dressing: mix the mustard, the remaining lemon juice, the oil, balsamic vinegar and garlic in a bowl. Whisk well with a fork and season. Toss the salad with the dressing, sprinkle with the chives and serve on a bed of frisée lettuce leaves. If served as a main course, accompany with boiled potatoes.

Chicken, Oyster Mushroom & Frisée Salad
with Pine-nuts & Sultanas,
and Warm Salad of Squid & Watercress
with Roasted Peanut Dressing
(page 88)

PASTA

TORTIGLIONI WITH ASPARAGUS & SUN-DRIED TOMATO PESTO

25 minutes

The Romans considered the asparagus an aphrodisiac: I'm sure they read more into the shape of this delicious vegetable than was necessary! Asparagus is at its best in Europe around May and June. If it is not available, substitute with mangetout. Serves 4.

salt & freshly ground black pepper
16–20 stems of asparagus, white base removed & stalks peeled
400 g/14 oz tortiglioni (slightly twisted pasta tubes)

For the pesto
170 g/6 oz sun-dried tomatoes
50 g/2 oz whole almonds
2 cloves of garlic
75 g/3 oz flat-leaf parsley, roughly chopped
zest of 1 lemon
100 ml/3.5 fl.oz olive oil
100 ml/3.5 fl.oz extra-virgin olive oil
50 g/2 oz Parmesan cheese, freshly grated
salt & freshly ground black pepper

5

4

1 Bring a large saucepan of salted water to the boil. Add the asparagus and blanch for 1 minute, then remove from the water with a perforated spoon and refresh in cold water. Drain well and slice.

10-12

2 Return the cooking water to the boil and cook the tortiglioni.

3 Make the pesto: place the sun-dried tomatoes, almonds, garlic, parsley and lemon zest in a food processor and whizz until all the ingredients are well blended, then steadily pour in the two oils while the machine is still running. Remove the mixture from the food processor and place in a bowl. Stir in the Parmesan and check the seasoning.

2-3

4 When the pasta is cooked, take 1½ cups of the hot water and gently mix it into the pesto. Add the asparagus and the well-drained pasta, mix well and serve.

2-3

TORCHIETTI *WITH* BROCCOLI, DOLCELATTE SAUCE & PECAN NUTS

Torchietti is one of the many dozens of pasta shapes produced. Experiment with different shapes as you will find that one sauce often complements a specific shape better than another. Serves 4.

25 minutes

salt & freshly ground black pepper
450 g/1 lb broccoli florets
150 g/5 oz mascarpone cheese
200 g/7 oz dolcelatte cheese, cut into cubes
2 tablespoons crème fraîche
1 tablespoon balsamic vinegar
1 tablespoon dry white wine
400 g/14 oz torchietti (twisted pasta curls)
50 g/2 oz pecan nuts

5

3-4

1 Bring a large saucepan of salted water to the boil. Blanch the broccoli in it for 1 minute, then remove with a perforated spoon, refresh under cold running water and set aside. Keep the hot water to cook the torchietti in.

4

2 In a heavy-based saucepan gently heat the mascarpone and dolcelatte cheese with the crème fraîche, vinegar and wine until well blended. Season.

10-12

3 Cook the pasta and when it is ready, drain well.

1-2

4 Bring the sauce to simmering point and add the broccoli. Toss the pasta in the sauce and serve sprinkled with the pecan nuts and plenty of freshly ground black pepper.

POPPY SEED & ALMOND PASTA

A simple, colourful and wonderfully delicious way of serving noodles. This dish evolved in the poverty-stricken peasant kitchens of Central Europe as a quick, easy-to-make, substantial and cheap stand-by.

The same simple dish can be made from other ingredients. Try using flaked hazelnuts, pecans or walnuts instead of the almonds. Or to make it more substantial and richer, omit the nuts and fold in 300 g/10 oz very fresh cottage cheese. Sprinkle with freshly grated Parmesan or any other strong-tasting cheese and finish with a few tablespoons of fresh thick cream.

Any wide egg noodles or pasta can be used for this dish, but my favourites are thickish wide continental noodles or wide tagliatelle. Serves 4.

20 minutes

500 g/1 lb 2 oz fresh tagliatelle
salt & freshly ground black pepper
a little oil
75 g/3 oz butter
75 g/3 oz black poppy seeds
75 g/3 oz flaked almonds
2 tablespoons finely chopped fresh parsley

5

1   Cook the pasta in plenty of salted water with a few drops of oil added. When it is ready, drain very thoroughly and keep warm.

8-10

2   Melt the butter in a heavy-based pan. Add the poppy seeds and almonds and fry until they begin to change colour and emit a pleasant nutty aroma. Add the drained pasta, mix well and heat through. Serve very hot, sprinkled with parsley.

5

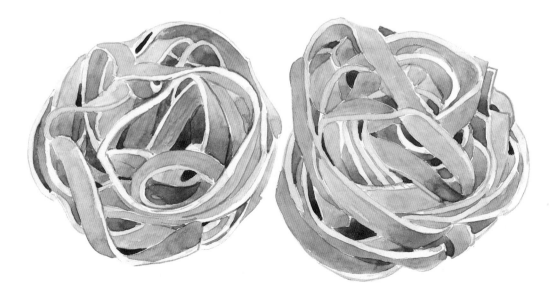

FETTUCCINE WITH SPINACH, MUSHROOM & GOAT'S CHEESE

Fresh goat's cheese (British or French) melted with crème fraîche makes a delicious creamy sauce for pasta, much tastier than double cream alone. Serves 4.

25 minutes

salt & freshly ground black pepper
100 g/4 oz unsalted butter
2 shallots, finely chopped
1 clove of garlic, finely chopped
275 g/10 oz chestnut button mushrooms, washed & sliced
juice of ½ lemon
2 tablespoons crème fraîche
100 g/4 oz fresh goat's cheese, cut into small chunks
170 g/6 oz fresh small-leaf or baby spinach, washed, drained & roughly chopped

10

400 g/14 oz fettuccine (ribbon noodles)

5

1 Bring a large saucepan of salted water to the boil.

2 Meanwhile, melt the butter in a frying pan. When it begins to sizzle, add the shallots and garlic and leave to colour for a couple of minutes, then add the mushrooms and lemon juice. Season and cook until most of the juice has evaporated.

4-5

3 Spoon the crème fraîche and goat's cheese into the pan. Leave to simmer over a low heat, stirring occasionally, until the cheese has melted, then add the spinach and leave to wilt in the sauce.

3-4

4 Cook the fettuccine. When it is ready, drain well, then toss in the sauce and serve with a final sprinkling of freshly ground black pepper.

4-5

THREE-MUSHROOM NOODLES

This dish is heaven: soft chewy noodles perfumed with three varieties of fungi. The most accessible combination is oyster, shitake and brown cap mushrooms. These are available in almost all big supermarkets. One can be more adventurous (and extravagant) and use wild mushrooms. Combinations of ceps, horn of plenty and Jew's ear or fresh or rehydrated black fungi, straw mushrooms and brown caps work very well.

In cranberry season add 75 g/3 oz lightly cooked cranberries just before serving. Their tartness complements the richness of the mushrooms well. Serves 4.

30 minutes

4 tablespoons peanut or sesame oil
100 g/4 oz onion or shallots, quartered
2 cloves of garlic, thickly sliced
300 g/10 oz brown cap mushrooms, wiped clean & sliced
200 g/7 oz oyster mushrooms, broken into chunks
100 g/4 oz fresh shitake, stems removed & sliced, or 50 g/2 oz dry shitake,
    rehydrated in warm water, stems removed & sliced
4 tablespoons dark soy sauce
400 ml/14 fl.oz vegetable stock
500 g/1 lb 2 oz fresh or dried Chinese egg noodles
salt

5

2 tablespoons chopped fresh dill, to garnish

(25)

1 If using dry shitake mushrooms, soak for 25 minutes in warm water before use.

2 Heat the oil in a wok or a heavy-based frying pan. Add the onion or shallots and the garlic and fry over a high heat until the mixture starts to brown. Add the mushrooms and continue frying until they begin to emit their juices. Add the soy sauce and fry for a minute or two, then add the stock. Bring to the boil, reduce the heat and simmer over a low heat for 10 minutes.

15

3 Prepare the noodles. If fresh, boil for 3 minutes, testing all the time – they should be tender but firm – then drain well. For dry noodles, see manufacturer's instructions.

3-10

4 Increase the heat under the mushrooms, add the drained noodles and cook, folding the noodles into the mushroom sauce, until almost all the liquid has evaporated and the noodles are glossy. Adjust the salt, sprinkle with dill and serve hot with a fresh salad.

3-5

MUSHROOM & PANCETTA PASTA

Mushroom madness spreads through Italy in spring and again in autumn. Woods are alive with the mushroom gatherers, and wild mushrooms have an extraordinary flavour and aroma, the mixture of which gets the taste buds going.

This dish tastes wonderful made from fresh porcini; but they are expensive even in Italy. A combination of brown cup and dried porcini works very well, and the dried funghi are now available in most supermarkets or in Italian grocers. Serves 4.

30 minutes

2 tablespoons olive oil
1 large onion, peeled & coarsely chopped
250 g/8 oz pancetta, coarsely diced
15 g/½ oz dried porcini, soaked in boiling water
    for 30 minutes
500 g/1 lb brown cup or large field mushrooms,
    wiped clean & thinly sliced
1 tablespoon dark soy sauce
400 ml/14 fl.oz chicken stock or water
salt & freshly ground black pepper
750 g/1½ lb fresh or dried tagliatelle or farfalle

to finish
grated zest of ½ lemon
2 tablespoons flat-leaf parsley, finely chopped
2 cloves of garlic, peeled & finely chopped
grated Parmesan cheese

5

1 Heat the oil in a heavy-based frying pan and add the onion. Fry until it starts to change colour. Add the pancetta and fry for a few more minutes.

5-6

2 Drain the porcini, and chop them finely. Add them to the pan with the sliced fresh mushrooms. Fry for 5 minutes longer, mixing well until the mushrooms have just softened.

7-10

3 Add the soy sauce and the stock, season and bring to the boil. Reduce the heat and simmer for about 15-20 minutes or until most of the liquid has evaporated.

17-22

4 Meanwhile, boil the pasta according to the manufacturer's instructions. Drain well and add to the pan, together with the lemon zest, parsley and garlic. Mix gently with a fork, heat through and serve immediately. Put a generous bowl of Parmesan cheese on the table.

10-12

PIPE WITH AUBERGINES, FRESH TOMATO, BASIL & RICOTTA

Ricotta is a by-product of cheese-making, obtained by reheating the whey, and it varies in texture depending on the richness of the milk used. Look for delicate flavours and a creamy texture. Serves 4.

30 minutes

2 aubergines
salt & freshly ground black pepper
6 tablespoons olive oil
400 g/14 oz pipe (pipe-shaped pasta)
1–2 tablespoons extra-virgin olive oil
1 medium red onion, finely chopped

1 clove of garlic, finely chopped
2 medium beef tomatoes, peeled & chopped
12 large basil leaves, roughly torn into pieces
225 g/8 oz ricotta, crumbled with a fork
4 tablespoons freshly grated Parmesan cheese

20-22

1 First prepare the aubergines. Cut them into cubes, sprinkle generously with salt and leave to drain for 20 minutes. Then wash off the salt and pat dry.

10-15

2 Heat a roasting pan with 3–4 tablespoons of the olive oil in a pre-heated oven at 230°C/450°F/Gas Mark 8 for a couple of minutes. When the oil is hot very carefully toss the cubes of aubergine in it and roast in the oven, stirring occasionally, for 10–15 minutes until golden and soft. Remove from the roasting pan and keep warm.

10-12

3 Meanwhile bring a large saucepan of salted water to the boil and cook the pipe.

5-6

4 While the pasta cooks, make the sauce: heat the remaining olive oil and the extra-virgin olive oil in a frying pan with the onion and garlic. Simmer for a couple of minutes, then add the tomatoes and seasoning. Cook for 5 minutes then add the aubergines.

2-3

5 When the pasta is ready, drain well and toss in the sauce. Lastly add the basil and sprinkle with the ricotta. Toss quickly but thoroughly and serve with a dusting of Parmesan.

FUSILLI WITH ROASTED PEPPERS, CAPERS & ANCHOVIES

Anchovies are often used in southern Italian cooking to enhance flavours. This type of sauce/dressing for pasta is usually served on the eve of religious celebrations which entail serious cooking – and serious eating – prior to a period of fasting. Serves 4.

30 minutes

2 red peppers
1 yellow pepper
2 tablespoons olive oil
400 g/14 oz fusilli (pasta twists)
2 tablespoons extra-virgin olive oil
5–6 anchovy fillets

2 cloves of garlic, finely chopped
1 tablespoon balsamic vinegar
1 tablespoon small capers, washed & squeezed dry
1 tablespoon flat-leaf parsley, finely chopped
1 tablespoon toasted breadcrumbs

5

20-25

1 Place the peppers in a roasting pan, drizzle with a little of the olive oil and roast in a pre-heated oven at 230°C/450°F/Gas Mark 8 for 15–20 minutes, or until most of the skins have blistered. Remove from the oven, place in a bowl, cover with cling-film and leave to cool slightly, then peel and cut the flesh into strips.

2-3

2 Bring a large saucepan of salted water to the boil and cook the fusilli.

2-3

3 Meanwhile, heat the two oils in a large frying pan with the anchovies and the garlic over a medium to low heat, stirring gently. When the anchovies dissolve into the sauce, add the vinegar, capers and the pepper strips.

12

4 When the pasta is ready, drain well and toss in the sauce with the parsley. Serve sprinkled with the breadcrumbs.

CONCHIGLIE WITH MUSSELS, COURGETTES & OLIVES

This recipe calls for a tin of chopped plum tomatoes as it is very difficult to buy ripe and flavoursome fresh plum tomatoes at market stalls or supermarkets. But if you are lucky do use fresh ones. Serves 4.

30 minutes

450 g / 1 lb fresh mussels, shells scrubbed & 'beards' removed
salt & freshly ground black pepper
3 tablespoons olive oil
1 medium onion, chopped
1 clove of garlic, finely chopped
2 medium courgettes, cut into bite-size pieces
1 x 400 g / 14 oz tin of chopped plum tomatoes
juice of 1 lemon
10 black olives, sliced
10 green olives, sliced
400 g / 14 oz conchiglie (pasta shells)
2 tablespoons chopped flat-leaf parsley

3

2 tablespoons extra-virgin olive oil

10-12

1   First cook the mussels: heat a heavy-based saucepan and when hot, put in the mussels and cover with a tight-fitting lid. Cook for about 5–10 minutes, shaking the pot vigorously, while holding the lid down firmly. When all the mussels have opened, remove from the heat and drain in a colander. Discard any that do not open.

2-3

2   Bring a large saucepan of salted water to the boil.

5-6

3   Shell the mussels, keeping some in the shell to garnish.

10-12

4   Heat the olive oil in a large frying pan. Add the onion and garlic and fry for a couple of minutes, then add the courgettes. Cook over a medium to high heat until golden, then add the chopped tomatoes and simmer for 10 minutes. Add the mussels, lemon juice, olives and seasoning.

10-12

5   Meanwhile, cook the conchiglie in the boiling water. When it is ready, drain well and toss in the sauce. Serve sprinkled with the parsley and the extra-virgin olive oil drizzled over.

GARGANELLI WITH LEEKS & SCALLOPS IN A SAFFRON SAUCE

25 minutes

Scallops are a favourite shellfish. When buying them, make sure they are fresh (firm flesh almost translucent), and do not overcook them as you may lose their flavour and sensual texture. Serves 4.

5

salt & freshly ground black pepper
3 leeks, sliced, washed & drained
400 g / 14 oz garganelli (hand-rolled pasta quills)
2 tablespoons dry white wine
½ teaspoon saffron strands

300 ml / 10 fl.oz double cream
3 tablespoons crème fraîche
grated rind of 1 lemon
1½ tablespoons finely chopped dill
12 king scallops

3-4

1 Bring a large saucepan of salted water to the boil. Blanch the leeks in it for 1 minute, then remove with a perforated spoon, refresh under cold running water and set aside.

10-12

2 Return to the boil and cook the garganelli.

7

3 Meanwhile, make the sauce: heat the wine with the saffron in a heavy-based frying pan and simmer until the liquid has reduced by half, then add the cream, crème fraîche, lemon rind and seasoning. Simmer for 3–4 minutes, then add the dill and leeks.

3

4 When the pasta is ready, drain well and toss in the sauce. While you toss the pasta, heat a dry frying pan over a high heat. Arrange the pasta on individual serving plates and sear the well-seasoned scallops in the hot frying pan for a minute or so on each side. Place on top of the prepared pasta and enjoy.

NOTE: If the scallops are very 'meaty', i.e. more than 2.5 cm/1 in thick, cut in half horizontally and proceed as instructed.

TAGLIOLINI WITH CRAB MEAT, SHALLOTS, LEMON GRASS & GINGER

15 minutes

East meets West: an almost typical cream sauce for a long-shaped pasta, given a slight edge with delicate and fresh oriental spicing. Serves 4.

salt & freshly ground black pepper
2 tablespoons olive oil
2 shallots, finely chopped
1 stick of lemon grass, finely chopped
50 g / 2 oz fresh ginger, peeled & grated
100 g / 4 oz brown crab meat
6 sun-dried tomatoes, cut into thin strips

juice of 1 lemon
2 tablespoons double cream
3 tablespoons crème fraîche
400 g / 14 oz tagliolini
170 g / 6 oz white crab meat
3 tablespoons chopped coriander leaves

5

3

1 Bring a large saucepan of salted water to the boil for the pasta.

3-4

2 Meanwhile, make the sauce: heat the oil in a frying pan, add the shallots, lemon grass and ginger and fry gently for a couple of minutes, then add the brown crab meat, sun-dried tomatoes and lemon juice and simmer for a minute or two. Add the cream, crème fraîche and seasoning.

2

3 While the tagliolini cooks, add the white crab meat and some of the coriander leaves to the sauce.

2-3

4 When the pasta is ready, drain well and toss in the sauce. Serve garnished with the remaining coriander leaves.

CHERRY TOMATO PASTA

A quick, delicious and spectacular pasta dish. It is based on the Italian classic, *pasta alla putanesca* – 'pasta prostitute-style'. It was so named because as it is quick and easy to make, the ladies of the night could cook it in short breaks between customers. The whole cherry tomatoes add a fresh, bright note to the pasta.

The most suitable tomatoes for the sauce – as for any tomato-based sauce – are either Italian plum, Provençal or beef. Serves 4.

25 minutes

3 tablespoons good olive oil
1 large onion, chopped
2–3 cloves of garlic, chopped
2 strips lemon or orange zest
500 g/1 lb 2 oz tomatoes, peeled, de-seeded & roughly chopped
a dash of white or red wine
a few drops of tabasco or ¼ teaspoon chilli powder (optional)
1 tablespoon capers
750 g/1½ lb large farfalle (pasta bows) or wide tagliatelle
225 g/8 oz cherry tomatoes
a little oil for brushing
salt & freshly ground black pepper
3 tablespoons chopped fresh basil
50–75 g/2–3 oz Parmesan cheese, shaved or grated
sprigs of fresh basil, to garnish

5

2-3

1 Heat the oil in a large heavy-based saucepan. Add the onion, garlic and lemon or orange zest and fry over a high heat until the mixture begins to take colour.

14-15

2 Add the chopped tomatoes, a dash of wine and tabasco or chilli, if used. Reduce the heat to medium and simmer for 10–12 minutes, mixing from time to time. Add the capers just before the sauce is ready.

8-15

3 Cook the pasta according to the packet instructions.

10

4 While the pasta and sauce are cooking, heat a dry frying pan. Brush the cherry tomatoes with olive oil, add to the hot pan and dry-roast until the skins begin to brown.

5

5 To serve, drain the pasta and toss with the sauce. Add the cherry tomatoes, salt, pepper and basil. Sprinkle the cheese on top and garnish with basil sprigs. Serve hot.

NOTE: Peeling tomatoes, although considered bothersome, is really very easy. Generally, it is best not to peel or over-process fresh ingredients, but peeling tomatoes seems necessary as many people object to pieces of tough, transparent skin floating in their sauce. To peel the tomatoes, cover for a minute or so in boiling water then rinse under the cold tap. The tomato skin should slip off very easily. After peeling, slice the tomatoes in half and squeeze out the seeds.

PASTA WITH SPICY ITALIAN SAUSAGES

Sausages are a most convenient fast food. Around the Mediterranean, where sausages were probably invented, they are used as instant flavouring for numerous stews and dishes. Smoked, spicy or mild sausages are added either fresh or dried to spike and flavour bland ingredients such as grain, beans, vegetables or pasta. The following recipe comes from Italy and calls for spicy-hot cooking sausage which is normally sold, in Italian delicatessens, under the name of 'Piquante' or peperone. If unobtainable any spicy *chorizo* type sausage will do. Serves 4.

30 minutes

3 tablespoons good olive oil
2 large onions, peeled & roughly chopped
4 fat cloves garlic, peeled & roughly chopped
3 strips lemon or orange zest
500 g / 1 lb spicy sausage, cut into large chunks
500 g / 1 lb plum tomatoes, peeled, de-seeded & roughly chopped
250 ml / 8 fl.oz robust red wine
salt & freshly ground pepper
750 g / 1½ lb pappardelle or wide fettucine
½ bunch of flat-leaf parsley, roughly chopped

5

1   Heat the oil in a large, heavy-based frying pan. Add the onion and garlic and fry for a few minutes until the onion starts to change colour. Add the lemon zest and sausage and fry for a few minutes more. Add the tomatoes and the wine, bring to the boil, reduce the heat and simmer over medium heat for about 20 minutes or until the sausages are cooked and the liquid much reduced.

25-30

2   Cook the pasta according to the manufacturer's directions. Pour the sauce over the pasta, sprinkle with plenty of parsley and serve immediately.

10-12

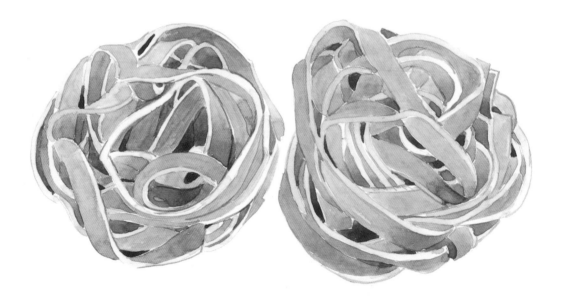

FARFALLE WITH FENNEL, SALMON & PINK PEPPERCORNS

Pink peppercorns have a delicate aromatic pip inside the pink shell, so when using ensure you grind them to a fine dust to make the most of their almost exotic perfume. Serves 4.

22 minutes

salt & freshly ground black pepper
1 large bulb of fennel, thinly sliced
400 g/14 oz farfalle (pasta bows)
225 g/8 oz mascarpone cheese
3 tablespoons crème fraîche
2 tablespoons dry white wine
1 tablespoon finely ground pink peppercorns
1 tablespoon finely chopped dill
2 tablespoons finely chopped chives

8

170 g/6 oz smoked salmon, cut into strips

3-4

1 Bring a large saucepan of salted water to the boil. Add the fennel and blanch for 1 minute. Remove with a perforated spoon, refresh under cold running water and set aside. Keep the hot water to cook the farfalle in.

8-10

2 While the pasta cooks, make the sauce: in a large saucepan gently heat the mascarpone with the crème fraîche and the wine. Season, then add the fennel, the pink pepper and half the herbs.

2

3 When the pasta is ready drain well, toss in the sauce and lastly add the salmon strips. Serve immediately, sprinkled with the remaining herbs.

PENNE WITH MERGEZ SAUSAGES, RED ONION, TOMATOES & ROCKET

Mergez are spicy beef or lamb sausages, originating from Algeria. They are also very popular in France. Serves 4.

25-30 minutes

salt & freshly ground black pepper
400 g/14 oz penne (pasta quills)
2 tablespoons olive oil
275 g/10 oz mergez sausages, cut into bite-size pieces
1 red onion, thinly sliced
2 tablespoons dry white wine
12 cherry tomatoes, halved
75 g/3 oz rocket leaves, thinly sliced

5

50 g/2 oz Parmesan cheese, freshly grated

10-12

1 Bring a large saucepan of salted water to the boil and cook the penne.

10-12

2 Heat the oil in a large frying pan. Add the mergez sausage and the onion and fry for a couple of minutes. Add the wine and simmer for 8–10 minutes, then add the tomatoes.

1-2

3 When the pasta is ready, drain well and toss in the sauce with the rocket. Mix well, check the seasoning and serve with the Parmesan.

SPAGHETTI WITH SMOKED DUCK, SPRING ONIONS & CHILLI

Try to find Spaghetti alla Chitarra for this dish – most well-known brands produce them. The Chitarra is a wooden rectangular frame with steel wires stretched across it. The rolled-out sheet of fresh pasta is pressed through the wires with a rolling pin to produce square spaghetti. Serves 4.

25 minutes

salt
400 g/14 oz spaghetti
3 tablespoons olive oil
1 red pepper, de-seeded & cut into thin strips
1–2 small red chillies, de-seeded & diced
1 clove of garlic, sliced
100 g/4 oz pak choy (Chinese spinach), washed & thinly sliced
170 g/6 oz smoked duck, sliced
1 tablespoon balsamic vinegar
1½ tablespoons ketjap manis (see page 158)
7 · *4 spring onions, sliced*

2 1 Bring a large saucepan of salted water to the boil and cook the spaghetti.

2 Heat the oil in a wok or large frying pan, add the pepper, chilli (use 2 if you like the dish hot), garlic and pak
3-4 choy and stir-fry for a couple of minutes over a high heat.

3 Add the duck, vinegar and ketjap manis. When the pasta is ready, drain well and stir into the sauce with the
12-14 spring onions. Toss well and serve. Chopsticks are optional!

GRILLED CHICKEN ESCALOPES
WITH *AROMATIC COUS COUS & YOGHURT DRESSING*

Couscous is made from the ground core of the durum wheat grain and is the staple diet of most north African countries. Serves 4.

30 minutes

200 g/7 oz couscous
200 ml/7 fl.oz boiling water
2 tablespoons extra-virgin olive oil
2 tablespoons finely chopped flat-leaf parsley
1 tablespoon finely chopped coriander
1 tablespoon finely chopped dill
1 tablespoon finely chopped chives
1 medium red onion, thinly sliced
1 medium red pepper, de-seeded & finely diced
salt & freshly ground black pepper
4 x 225 g/8 oz chicken breasts, split in half horizontally

For the yogurt dressing
4 tablespoons Greek strained yogurt
1 clove of garlic, finely chopped
1 tablespoon extra-virgin olive oil
juice of 1 lemon
salt & freshly ground black pepper

10

1   1 First make the dressing by mixing together all the ingredients. Cover and set aside.

      2 Prepare the couscous: pour the hot salted water over the couscous in a mixing bowl and leave to stand for 3–4 minutes until all the water has been absorbed. Add the oil, herbs, onion and pepper and keep stirring with a fork or metal spoon until all the ingredients are well mixed but the couscous grains are separated. Check the
5   seasoning and set aside.

      3 Heat a grilling pan. Season the chicken escalopes and when the pan is hot, grill for 4–5 minutes on each side or
8-10   until done.

1   4 Arrange the grilled escalopes on the cous cous and serve with the yogurt dressing.

CHICKEN BREAST COOKED WITH PEPPERS & SUN-DRIED TOMATOES

This flavoursome dish is delicious either hot or served cold as a delightful summer lunch dish. Rice or burgul pilaf goes well with the rich Mediterranean tang of the peppers. Serves 4.

25 minutes

4 tablespoons good olive oil
1 large onion, peeled & thinly sliced
4 cloves of garlic, peeled & roughly sliced
2 red peppers, de-seeded & sliced into a fine julienne
2 green peppers, de-seeded & sliced into a fine julienne
75 g / 3 oz sun-dried tomatoes in oil, sliced into thin julienne
300 ml / 12 fl. oz boiling chicken stock or water
500 g / 1 lb chicken breast, sliced into 1-cm / ½-in strips
salt & freshly ground black pepper
2 tablespoons chopped coriander leaves

5

1 Heat the oil in a heavy-based frying pan and add the onion, garlic and the peppers. Fry over a medium heat for a few minutes or until the onion starts to change colour. Add the tomatoes and their oil, together with the stock, bring to the boil, reduce the heat and simmer, covered, for 10 minutes.

15

2 Season the chicken with salt and pepper. Increase the heat of the pepper and tomato mixture, add the chicken and go on cooking, stirring all the time, for about 5 minutes or until the chicken is done and most of the liquid has evaporated. Check the seasoning and sprinkle with coriander and serve.

5-7

CHICKEN COOKED WITH OLIVES & ORANGE

The combination of tart orange with the salty bitterness of the olives and the chicken is magic. Serve it hot with either rice, burgul or couscous. Serves 4.

30+ minutes

100 g/4 oz broken green olives (see below)
4-6 boneless chicken breasts, skin removed
100 g/4 oz flour seasoned with salt,
*   freshly ground black pepper and 1 teaspoon paprika*
4 tablespoons olive oil
1 large onion, peeled & finely chopped
100 ml/4 fl. oz dry white wine
250 ml/8 fl. oz chicken stock or water
juice of 3 tart oranges
grated zest of 1 orange
1 teaspoon freshly ground coriander
salt & freshly ground black pepper

5

2 tablespoons coriander leaves for decoration

20   1 Soak the olives in boiling water for 20 minutes.

2-3   2 With a sharp knife make 3 gashes in each chicken breast and dip them in the seasoned flour. Set aside.

3 Heat the oil in a shallow, heavy-based pan. Add the onion and chicken breast and fry for a few minutes until onion starts to turn colour. Add the wine, chicken stock, juice, zest and ground coriander. Bring to the boil,
25   reduce the heat and simmer gently for 20 minutes.

4 Add the olives and the seasoning, increase the heat and boil rapidly for about 5 minutes until the sauce is
5   reduced and shiny. Serve with rice, couscous or burgul decorated with chopped coriander leaves.

DUCK BREAST WITH ROASTED RED ONION & BEETROOT
SERVED WITH A GINGER SAUCE

When using duck breast try not to overcook the meat, for the more you cook it the tougher it will become. Before slicing and serving allow a few minutes 'resting' time – the meat will remain pink, tender and juicy. Serves 4.

30 minutes

1 tablespoon olive oil
4 red onions, peeled & cut into segments
4 raw beetroots, peeled & cut into segments
salt & freshly ground black pepper
100 ml/3⅓ fl.oz red wine
4 x 170 g/6 oz duck breasts, skin scored, patted dry & rubbed with salt
50 g/2 oz fresh ginger, peeled & cut into thin strips
2 tablespoons balsamic vinegar

5

80 g/3 oz unsalted butter, cut into small cubes

15-20

1 Heat the oil in a roasting pan. Add the onions and beetroot, season and moisten with a couple of spoonfuls of the wine. Cover with foil and bake in a pre-heated oven at 220°C/425°F/Gas Mark 7 for 15–20 minutes.

10-12

2 When the vegetables are half-way through their cooking, heat a frying pan and when it is hot, sear the duck breasts skin-side down for a couple of minutes, then turn over and cook for a further minute or two. Transfer to a baking tray and cook in the oven for a further 6–8 minutes, turning occasionally.

1

3 Remove the duck breasts from the oven and keep warm.

4

4 Remove the pan with the vegetables, place on the stove and remove the foil. Turn the heat up and add the ginger, remaining red wine and vinegar to the pan. Cook for a couple of minutes, then remove the vegetables and keep warm.

3

5 Let the juices in the pan reduce slightly, then gradually work in the butter, stirring continuously so that all the ingredients are well blended.

2-3

6 Place the beetroot and onions on a serving plate, slice the duck and arrange on the vegetables. Spoon around the sauce and serve.

BREAST OF BARBARY DUCK IN TAMARIND SAUCE

Barbary ducks are said to have originated in the Barbary Mountains of North Africa; in fact they were developed in the South of France and are now available at the speciality meat counters of most big supermarkets.

Tamarind or Indian date is the sour pulp which surrounds the seeds of the tamarind tree. It is sold in most Indian and oriental stores, either as a compressed slab or as a paste. The paste is the easiest to use as, in the other form, the tamarind needs to be soaked in hot water and sieved to get rid of the seeds. Tamarind was introduced to the eastern Mediterranean from India and it was popularly used as a souring agent and as the base of many sauces, refreshing drinks and sorbets. Its fruity tang makes it ideal for the gamey flavour of the Barbary duck.

30 minutes

This is an adaptation of an ancient Italian recipe. Serves 4.

4-6 boneless breasts of Barbary duck
1 tablespoon fragrant honey
3 tablespoons good olive oil
100 g/4 oz shallots, peeled & quartered
2 cloves of garlic, peeled & roughly sliced
2 tablespoons tamarind paste
2 teaspoons honey or brown sugar
150 ml/6 fl.oz chicken stock
50 g/2 oz fruity red wine
50 g/2 oz currants

5

salt & freshly ground black pepper

1

1 Heat the grill to maximum.

10

2 Make 3 deep slashes in each breast and brush with the honey. Grill the duck breasts for 4 minutes on each side, place on a warmed dish, and keep hot.

20

3 Heat the oil in a heavy-based frying pan. Add the shallots and garlic and fry until the shallots start to change colour. Mix the tamarind together with the honey, stock and wine and add to the pan. Add the currants, season and bring to the boil. Reduce the heat and simmer for 15 minutes.

10

4 Increase the heat, and boil rapidly for about 3-4 minutes until the sauce is thickened and shiny. Add the duck and continue cooking for a minute or two, frequently turning in the sauce. If you like your duck well done continue cooking until done to your liking, for about a further 5 minutes.

ROASTED QUAILS ON SPICED BASMATI RICE
WITH A SHERRY VINEGAR SAUCE

Quails are deliciously tasty and quick to cook. To enjoy them best – use your hands. (Fingerbowls essential!) Serves 4.

30 minutes

3 tablespoons olive oil
100 g/4 oz unsalted butter
8 quails, washed & patted dry
salt & freshly ground black pepper
150 g/5 oz basmati rice, washed & drained
2 shallots, finely sliced
1 teaspoon ground coriander seeds
½ cinnamon stick, crushed
1 small red pepper, de-seeded & finely diced
1 small red chilli, de-seeded & finely diced
2 tablespoons sherry vinegar
3 tablespoons crème fraîche
coriander leaves, to garnish

5

20

1 Heat 2 tablespoons of the oil with 25 g/1 oz of the butter in a roasting pan. When the butter begins to foam fry the quails on all sides until golden. Season and roast in a pre-heated oven at 220°C/425°F/Gas Mark 7 for about 15 minutes, turning the birds occasionally.

12

2 Meanwhile, prepare the rice: bring a large saucepan of salted water to the boil and cook the rice for about 10 minutes, until just tender. When it is ready, drain well, rinse under cold running water and set aside.

4

3 Heat the remaining oil and butter in a frying pan. When they begin to sizzle, add the shallots, coriander, cinnamon, pepper and chilli. Fry for a couple of minutes, then add the rice and mix well. Check the seasoning and keep warm.

5

4 Remove the cooked quails from the roasting pan and keep warm. Drain any excess fat from the roasting pan and place the pan over a high heat. Deglaze with the vinegar and leave to simmer and reduce for a minute or so. Then stir in the crème fraîche, check the seasoning and cook for a couple of minutes, to thicken.

1

5 Place the rice on serving plates, arrange the quails on top, spoon over the sauce and garnish with the coriander leaves.

NOTE: The sherry sauce may need to be passed through a sieve.

ESCALOPES OF VEAL ON ROASTED FIELD MUSHROOMS & WILTED SPINACH SERVED WITH ANCHOVY BUTTER

Blending different fresh herbs or flavourings with butter is an easy way to preserve perfumes and essences. A slice of flavoured butter can turn plain grilled meat or fish into an interesting meal. Serves 4.

30 minutes

150 g/5 oz soft unsalted butter
6 anchovy fillets in oil, drained & chopped to a pulp
juice of ½ lemon
salt & freshly ground black pepper
4 large flat field mushrooms, stalks removed
2 tablespoons olive oil
50 g/2 oz cold butter
1 small clove of garlic, finely chopped
400 g/14 oz spinach leaves, washed, stalks removed & roughly chopped
5   *4 x 200 g/7 oz veal escalopes*

2   1 First make the anchovy butter: using a wooden spoon blend together in a bowl the soft butter, anchovy pulp and lemon juice. Season, mix well and refrigerate.

15-20   2 Place the mushrooms in a roasting pan. Sprinkle with the oil and season. Bake in a pre-heated oven at 220°C/425°F/Gas Mark 8 for 15–20 minutes or until soft right through.

3-4   3 Remove the mushrooms from the oven and slice. Melt the cold butter in the roasting pan with the garlic, add the spinach and allow to wilt then add the sliced mushrooms and mix well.

2-3   4 While the mushrooms and spinach are cooking, heat a grilling pan. Season the veal escalopes and grill for a minute or so on each side.

1   5 Serve the veal arranged on the vegetables, with a curl of anchovy butter on each serving.

VEAL IN ANCHOVY & CAPER SAUCE

Veal is much loved by the Italians, but I find the butter and cream which are associated with veal cooking much too heavy. The following is an adaptation of an Italian classic with neither. Served on a bed of pasta it makes a light, healthy and delicious main course. Serves 4

40 minutes

500 g/1 lb veal escalopes, thinly sliced but not pounded
flour for dusting
4 tablespoons good olive oil
1 large onion, peeled & coarsely chopped
3 cloves garlic, peeled & coarsely chopped
2 tablespoons capers, rinsed & coarsely chopped
1 x 50 g/2 oz tin of anchovies, drained & roughly chopped
1-2 strips of lemon zest
500 g/1 lb plum tomatoes, skinned, de-seeded & roughly chopped
150 ml/6 fl.oz white wine
salt & freshly ground pepper
500 g/1 lb tagliatelle or spaghetti

5

3 tablespoons chopped flat-leaf parsley

2

1 Slice the escalopes into thick strips about 2.5 cm/1 in wide. Dust with flour.

8-12

2 Heat 3 tablespoons of the oil in a heavy bottomed frying pan. Add the veal slices, a few at a time, and fry over a medium heat for about 2–3 minutes on each side or until nicely browned. Do not over-crowd the pan. Lift them into a warmed dish and keep warm..

15-20

3 Add the zest of the oil, together with onion, garlic, capers, anchovies and lemon zest. Fry for a few minutes, mixing frequently. Add the tomatoes and the wine, season and bring to the boil. Reduce the heat and simmer for about 10–15 minutes.

8-12

4 Cook the pasta according to the manufacturer's instructions. When ready drain well and keep hot. Add the escalopes to the simmering sauce, heat through, season and arrange on a bed of pasta. Sprinkle with parsley and serve.

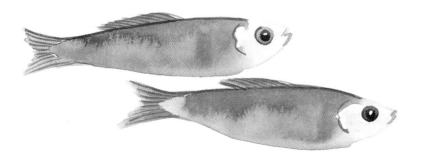

GRILLED SIRLOIN STEAK WITH PEPPERS, AUBERGINES & SALSA VERDE

30+ minutes

This tasty relish is a classic northern Italian recipe traditionally served with boiled meats. It is quite suitable for grills as well. Serves 4.

1 large aubergine
salt & freshly ground black pepper
5 tablespoons olive oil
2 red peppers, de-seeded & quartered
2 yellow peppers, de-seeded & quartered
2–3 cloves of garlic, crushed
4 x 200 g/7 oz sirloin steak

For the salsa verde
1 bunch of flat-leaf parsley
50 g/2 oz day-old bread, crusts removed
100 g/4 oz gherkins, well drained
100 g/4 oz capers, squeezed dry
4 anchovy fillets
2 cloves of garlic
5 tablespoons extra-virgin olive oil
salt & freshly ground black pepper

5

20

1 First prepare the aubergine. Cut in half lengthways, then crossways into thin segments. Sprinkle generously with salt and leave to drain for 20 minutes.

1

2 Heat two-thirds of the oil in a roasting pan. Wash the aubergine to remove the salt, pat dry and add to the pan. Season.

15

3 Heat the remaining oil in a second roasting pan and add the peppers and garlic. Season. Roast both pans of vegetables in a pre-heated oven at 230°C/450°F/Gas Mark 8 for about 15 minutes, tossing occasionally.

1

4 Meanwhile, make the salsa by blending all the ingredients in a food processor. Check the seasoning and set aside.

5-10

5 Heat a grilling pan. Season the steaks and when the pan is hot, grill them to your preferred taste.

1

6 Serve the steaks with the hot vegetables and the salsa verde. New potatoes or a crisp salad and crusty bread would complete this dish perfectly.

LAMB STEAKS WITH FRESH APRICOT SAUCE

The combination of young tender lamb and apricots is magical. It appears in many forms around the Mediterranean. In North Africa it is made into a delicious tagine (stew) and in Jerusalem there is a recipe in which apricots are stuffed with minced lamb and cooked in a sweet and sour sauce.

The following dish is a modern interpretation of this age old combination. When fresh apricots are not in season, dried apricots which have previously soaked in hot water can be used. Serves 4.

25 minutes

2 tablespoons honey
2 tablespoons olive oil
4-6 lamb steaks, each weighing about 150 g/6 oz
salt & freshly ground black pepper

for the sauce
500 g/1 lb fresh apricots, kernels removed or
150 g/6 oz dried apricots
1-2 tablespoons honey (to taste)
2 tablespoons chopped fresh mint (or 1 tablespoon dried)
a few drops of lemon juice
1/2 teaspoon grated lemon zest
salt & freshly ground black pepper

5

a few sprigs of fresh mint for decoration

12-15

1　Heat the grill to maximum. Mix the honey with the oil and brush over the steaks. Season with salt and pepper. Grill at a high heat for 4–5 minutes each side. This will result in medium rare lamb steaks; if you like your lamb well done, grill for a few minutes more.

3-5

2　Put all the sauce ingredients into a food processor and process into a smooth purée.

1

3　Decorate each steak with a sprig of mint and serve on a pool of sauce.

BARBECUED SHISH KEBABS

Mediterranean evenings are often associated with the sweet smell of jasmine and the irresistible, appetising aroma of barbecuing meats. Sweet herbs and aromatic woods are used to impart special flavour to anything cooked on them.

A barbecue is a full meal which can include barbecued vegetables, mushrooms and cheese to start with, followed by fish, seafood, meat and sausages and all served with fresh salads, bread, and, depending where you come from, large quantities of wine, ouzo, raki or beer.

Modern gas barbecues are convenient and easier to use, but if you have the time, do it the traditional way with good hardwood coals. And do experiment with different aromatic herbs such as rosemary branches, thyme or even lavender. These should be placed on the hot coals just before adding the meats.

This recipe is of Lebanese origin. Serve with Tahina sauce (page 257), a pilav of burgul or rice for a main course or lunch. Serves 4.

30 minutes

1 medium onion, peeled & quartered
1 small clove of garlic, mashed
½ bunch flat-leaf parsley, stems removed
1-2 green chillies, trimmed & de-seeded (optional)
750 g / 1½ lb ground lean lamb or beef
2-3 tablespoons good olive oil
a pinch of cinnamon
¼ teaspoon allspice
¼ teaspoon ground cardamom (optional)
salt & freshly ground pepper

5

2-3

1 Place the onion, garlic and chilli (if used) in a food processor and process, starting and stopping the machine, until finely chopped but not puréed

3

2 Transfer into a mixing bowl, add the rest of the ingredients and mix very well.

16-20

3 With wet hands shape into thick kebabs. Either grill or barbecue for about 7–8 minutes each side for a rare kofta, 10 for a medium or longer still if liked. Serve immediately with a pilav, fresh salad and Tahina sauce.

COFTAS COOKED IN TAHINA SAUCE

A delicious dish of Lebanese origin which can be served either as a main course or as a appetising starter. Serves 4.

30+ minutes

1 medium onion, peeled
2 cloves of garlic, peeled
½ bunch flat-leaf parsley, leaves only
500 g/1 lb raw minced lamb
50 g/2 oz breadcrumbs
1 egg
½ teaspoon allspice
salt & freshly ground black pepper
1 quantity of tahina sauce (see page 257), diluted with 50 g/2 oz of water
1 tablespoon each of pine nuts & parsley for decoration

5

1

1 Heat the grill to maximum and heat the oven to 220°C/425°F/Gas Mark 7.

2 Put the onion, garlic and parsley into the food processor and process, turning the machine on and off, until roughly chopped. Transfer into a large mixing bowl and add the rest of the ingredients except the tahina and decoration. Mix well.

3-5

3 Wet your hands and shape the mixture into 5 cm/2 in coftas, like round sausages. Grill the coftas for 4-5 minutes each side. They should just remain pink inside.

15

4 Arrange the coftas in a greased, oven proof dish. Pour the tahina over and bake for about 10 minutes or until the tahina is bubbling and starts to brown. Decorate with pine-nuts which have previously browned in a little oil and parsley. Serve hot with rice or burgul.

10-12

LAMB COFTAS COOKED WITH LEMON & CUMIN

Around the Mediterranean meat used to be an expensive commodity. Large joints were cooked only for special celebrations or on Sunday. For everyday food many techniques of 'stretching' meat were developed. Minced meat was bulked with either bread or rice and burgul. The addition of chopped herbs and vegetables to the mixture produces light, healthier coftas, being reduced in saturated fat content. The following recipe comes from Morocco. Serves 4.

30 minutes

1 large onion, sliced
1 large bunched of flat-leaf parsley, tough stems removed
2-3 sticks of green celery (see below)
500 g/1 lb very lean lamb, minced
1 egg
2 tablespoons virgin olive oil
75 g/3 oz fresh breadcrumbs or soaked burgul
¼ teaspoon whole cumin seeds
olive oil for frying

for the sauce
3 tablespoons olive oil
¼ teaspoon whole cumin seeds
1 medium onion, finely chopped
1 clove of garlic, finely chopped
250 ml/8 fl.oz stock or dry white wine
2 teaspoons tomato purée
1 small lemon, peeled & sliced into small cubes
salt & freshly ground black pepper

1 tablespoon chopped parsley for decoration

10

1
1   Heat the grill to maximum.

2-3
2   Put the onion, parsley and celery into a food processor and process, switching the machine on and off, until the mixture is chopped but not puréed. Transfer the mixture into a mixing bowl and add the rest of the main ingredients. Mix thoroughly.

15
3   Shape into 12 thickish patties and grill for about 5 minutes on each side. The coftas should remain slightly pink inside.

7-8
4   Meanwhile, to prepare the sauce: heat the oil in a heavy-based frying pan. Add the cumin and fry over high heat for a second or two. Add the onion and the garlic and continue frying until the onion starts to change colour. Add the remaining ingredients, bring to the boil and boil for 5 minutes.

2
5   When the coftas are ready pour the boiling sauce over them. Decorate with chopped parsley and serve immediately accompanied by rice burgul or a salad.

NOTE: Dark green leaf celery is available in many Greek, Turkish and Indian shops. It has a strong celery flavour and is used for cooking rather than eating raw. If unavailable the 'American' variety will do.

LAMB CUTLETS ON A WARM TOMATO & ARTICHOKE SALAD

20 minutes

Choose well-trimmed cutlets with dark red meat, unless you are buying new season lamb. Serves 4.

12 lamb cutlets
salt & freshly ground black pepper
1 tablespoon olive oil
50 g/2 oz unsalted butter
1 sprig of fresh rosemary
4 marinated artichokes, cut into segments (see page 89)
1 clove of garlic, finely chopped
4 plum tomatoes, quartered, de-seeded & cut into segments

5

150 g/5 oz spinach leaves washed, drained & roughly chopped

1

1 Season the cutlets.

2 Heat the oil and butter with the rosemary in a large frying pan. When the butter begins to foam, sear the cutlets on both sides. Remove them from the pan with the rosemary and arrange on a baking tray. Cook in a pre-heated oven at 220°C/425°F/Gas Mark 7 for 5–6 minutes or longer if you prefer your lamb not quite pink.

10

3 Meanwhile, return the frying pan to the heat and bring back to sizzling point. Add the artichokes, garlic and tomatoes and quickly toss in the cooking juices. Add the spinach and warm through, checking the seasoning.

3

4 Distribute the warm salad on individual serving dishes and arrange the cutlets on top. Serve with baked potatoes or buttered basmati rice. Do not accompany with mint sauce!

2

Ragoût of Rabbit, Leeks & Green Lentils (page 159), and Lamb Cutlets on a Warm Tomato & Artichoke Salad

GRILLED LIVER ON A BED OF ROCKET LEAVES

Balsamic vinegar is obtained from ageing cooked concentrated must (grape juice) for seven to fifty or more years. The juice is kept in barrels or kegs made from different woods. As it ages the must thickens into a precious flavour-enhancing ingredient. Serves 4.

15 minutes

1½ medium red onions, finely diced
2 plum tomatoes, quartered, de-seeded & diced
1 tablespoon finely chopped chives
4 tablespoons extra-virgin olive oil
2 tablespoons balsamic vinegar
salt & freshly ground black pepper
450 g/1 lb calves' liver, sliced
150 g/5 oz rocket leaves, washed & drained

5

1

1 Make the salsa: in a bowl combine the onion, tomato, chives, oil and vinegar. Mix well and season. Set aside.

4

2 Season the liver. Heat a grilling pan and when the pan is very hot, grill the liver slices on both sides to your preferred taste.

3

3 Arrange the grilled liver on the rocket leaves (the heat of the liver will wilt the salad slightly) and spoon on the salsa. Serve with a warm potato salad.

SAUTÉ OF CHICKEN LIVERS & SHALLOTS ON SAGE POLENTA

The Romans cooked polenta made with a lesser kind of wheat and served it with meat stews. When Caesar's troops invaded Britain they brought the recipe with them but began to use a local grain – oats – leaving the Britons the tradition of porridge! Serves 4.

15 minutes

1 tablespoon olive oil
80 g/3 oz butter
4 shallots, sliced
225 g/8 oz button mushrooms, sliced
650 g/1½ lb chicken livers
1 tablespoon red wine
1½ tablespoons balsamic vinegar
salt & freshly ground black pepper

For the polenta
1.2 litres/2¼ pints milk
75 g/3 oz butter
1 clove of garlic, finely chopped
6 sage leaves, finely sliced
salt & freshly ground black pepper
250 g/9 oz instant polenta

5

1 First make the polenta: heat the milk in a saucepan with the butter, garlic, sage and seasoning. When it comes to the boil, lower the heat and pour in the polenta, stirring continuously. Cook, still stirring, for 1–2 minutes, then remove from the heat and keep warm. (The instructions on the polenta packet will require less liquid, but for this recipe follow the above method.)

1-2

2 Heat the oil and half the butter in a large frying pan. When the butter begins to foam, add the shallots and mushrooms and cook over a high heat for a couple of minutes. Remove the mushrooms and shallots with a perforated spoon and keep warm.

3

3 Bring the fat in the pan to sizzling point again and toss in the chicken livers, searing well on all sides. Return the vegetables to the frying pan, add the wine and vinegar and cook for a couple of minutes. Season and blend in the remaining butter. Spoon the polenta on to a serving dish, making a well in the centre. Arrange the livers with their sauce in the well and serve.

5

CHICKEN LIVER PILAFF

This pilaff is a delicious and subtle concoction of crunchy nuts and melting chicken liver. With a green-leaf salad it makes a delightful summer main course. Serves 4.

30 minutes

5 tablespoons olive oil or butter
350 g/14 oz long grain rice
1 litre/2 pints boiling chicken stock or water
50 g/2 oz sultanas
50 g/2 oz almonds
50 g/2 oz pine-nuts
300 g/12 oz chicken liver, sliced into
*   2.5 cm/1 in pieces*
1 large onion, peeled & thinly sliced
salt & freshly ground black pepper
5
2 tablespoons chopped dill

22-25

1   Heat 2 tablespoons of the oil in a heavy-based pan, add the rice and fry over high heat for a minute or two or until the rice starts changing colour and becomes opaquely white. Add the boiling stock and sultanas and bring to the boil. Reduce the heat, cover and simmer for 15-20 minutes or until the liquid has been absorbed and the rice is tender.

8

2   Heat the rest of the oil in a heavy-based frying pan, add the almonds and pine-nuts and fry for a minute or two until the nuts are nicely brown. Lift out and reserve. Add the livers and onion and fry for about 5 minutes until the liver is just cooked; the inside should remain pink and juicy. Season with salt and pepper.

2

3   Fold the nuts, liver mixture and dill into the rice, mix and fluff up with a fork, and serve immediately.

BURGUL PILAV

Burgul, mistakenly known as cracked wheat, is probably the most ancient convenience food. It is made from pre-cooked and dried wheat and, although this recipe *is* cooked, needs no cooking. Burgul is used a lot in the eastern part of the Mediterranean. Serves 4.

30+ minutes

3 tablespoons olive oil
1 small onion, chopped
300 g / 12 oz coarse grained burgul
750 ml / 1½ pints boiling water

3

Salt to taste

2-3

1   Heat the oil in a shallow pan. Add the onion and fry gently until soft and golden.

2   Add the burgul and continue frying, stirring frequently, for 2–3 minutes or until it begins to change colour. Add the boiling water and salt and stir well. Bring to the boil, reduce the heat and cover tightly. Simmer very gently for 15–20 minutes or until all the water is absorbed. Leave to rest, covered, for 10 minutes and serve.

30

MEDALLIONS OF PORK IN SPICY COATING
WITH A WARM SALAD OF CRISPY VEGETABLES

Amongst the ingredients for this recipe you will find ketjap manis, a sweet thick Indonesian soy sauce. Use sparingly in marinades, sauces and dressings for a light oriental flavouring. Serves 4.

30 minutes

100 g/4 oz plain flour
1 teaspoon ground cumin
½ teaspoon ground coriander
salt & freshly ground black pepper
170 g/6 oz breadcrumbs
3 tablespoons sesame seeds
1 egg
2 tablespoons water
2–3 pork tenderloins, weighing in total about 600 g/1¼ lb,
    cut into thick slices & lightly beaten into medallions
5 tablespoons olive oil
1 tablespoon ketjap manis
1 tablespoon balsamic vinegar
2 tablespoons extra-virgin olive oil
1 clove of garlic, finely chopped
50 g/2 oz fresh ginger, peeled & grated
5 spring onions, thinly sliced
1 red pepper, de-seeded & cut into batons
1 yellow pepper, de-seeded & cut into batons
170 g/6 oz mangetout, topped & tailed

10

75 g/3 oz unsalted butter

1-2

1 Mix the flour with the cumin, coriander and seasoning. Mix the breadcrumbs with the sesame seeds. Whisk the egg with the water.

1-2

2 Toss the pork medallions in the seasoned flour, then dip in the egg wash, lastly coat with the breadcrumbs. Set aside.

5

3 Heat two tablespoons of the olive oil in a wok or large frying pan. While the oil heats up, mix together in a large bowl the ketjap manis, vinegar, extra-virgin olive oil, garlic, ginger and spring onions, and season. When the oil in the wok is almost smoking, carefully toss in the peppers and mangetout and stir-fry for a couple of minutes. Then tip into the prepared dressing in the bowl, mix well and set aside.

7

4 Heat the remaining oil with the butter in a large frying pan. When the butter begins to foam, fry the medallions for 3–4 minutes on each side.

2

5 Serve the medallions with the prepared vegetables. Rice or noodles would make a suitable accompaniment.

RAGOÛT OF RABBIT, LEEKS & GREEN LENTILS WITH WHOLEGRAIN MUSTARD

Rabbit meat is not a favourite in the British repertoire, which is a pity as it is tastier than most chicken and low in cholesterol. Serves 4.

30 minutes

200 g/7 oz green lentils, previously soaked for 10–15 minutes
1 tablespoon plain flour
salt & freshly ground black pepper
700 g/1½ lb rabbit, boned & cut into small chunks
50 g/2 oz unsalted butter
2 tablespoons olive oil
2–3 leeks, sliced, washed & drained
1 clove of garlic, finely chopped
2 tablespoons wholegrain mustard
2–3 tablespoons dry white wine
150 ml/5 fl.oz hot chicken stock or water
1 tablespoon balsamic vinegar
150 ml/5 fl.oz double cream
1 tablespoon chopped flat-leaf parsley

5

15-20 1 Bring a saucepan of water to the boil. Drain the lentils and cook for 15–20 minutes until just soft.

2-3 2 Meanwhile, start to prepare the ragoût. Season the flour and toss the rabbit pieces in it. Shake off any excess.

3 Heat the butter with the oil in a large saucepan. When the butter begins to foam, add the rabbit, leeks and garlic and fry for a couple of minutes. Then add the mustard, wine and stock or water. Season, then simmer for *8-10* 8–10 minutes.

4 When the lentils are ready, drain well. Add to the cooked ragoût and mix thoroughly. Add the vinegar and *3* cream, check the seasoning and lastly stir in the parsley.

2 5 Serve with crusty bread or steamed new potatoes and a crisp salad.

TUNA SERVED WITH PEPPER & OLIVE SAUCE

Since antiquity the dark, veal-like flesh of the tuna has been admired all over the Mediterranean. This French recipe is typical of the Côte d'Azur.

Fresh tuna should be treated carefully; when cooked for too long the flesh becomes dry and unpleasant. Therefore cook it until pink, rather than grey, just like lamb or beef.

If fresh tuna is not available, sword fish, which is plentiful in the sea all over the region, can be used instead. Serves 4.

30 minutes

4-6 tuna steaks each weighing about 150 g/6 oz
50 g/2 oz seasoned flour for dredging
4 tablespoons good olive oil
1 clove of garlic, peeled & crushed
1 red pepper, sliced into a thin julienne
3 anchovy fillets, chopped
100 g/4 oz black olives, pitted & chopped
100 ml/4 fl.oz stock
salt & freshly ground black pepper
juice of ½ a lemon
5
3 tablespoons dill or flat-leaf parsley, chopped

1

1 Dip the tuna steaks in the seasoned flour.

2 Heat half the oil in a heavy-based frying pan, add the tuna and fry over high heat for 2 minutes. Turn the steaks over and fry for a further 2 minutes. Remove and keep warm.
5

3 Add the rest of the oil and the garlic and red pepper and fry for a minute or two until the garlic starts to change colour. Add the anchovies, olives and the stock, and bring to the boil. Reduce the heat and simmer for about 10 minutes.
15

4 Increase the heat, add the tuna steaks and cook over a high heat for 4–5 minutes. Baste the steaks frequently with the cooking liquid. If you like your tuna well done continue to cook until the flesh is just flaking. Immediately before serving, season and sprinkle with the lemon juice and the chopped herbs.
5-7

ROASTED JOHN DORY WITH ROASTED TOMATO & OLIVE SALSA

John Dory is also known as St Peter's fish. The 'Fisher of Men' is said to have picked out a specimen from the day's catch to throw back into the sea, leaving the imprints of his thumb on one side of the fish and his forefinger on the other. To this day the silver-grey fish bears the marks on its skin. Serves 4.

25 minutes

2 tablespoons olive oil
25 g/1 oz unsalted butter
4 x 170 g/6 oz John Dory fillets
4–6 plum tomatoes, quartered
salt & freshly ground black pepper
2 tablespoons extra-virgin olive oil
2 lemons, halved

For the salsa
75 g/3 oz black olives, pitted, rinsed,
  drained & chopped
75 g/3 oz green olives, pitted, rinsed,
  drained & chopped
1 clove of garlic, finely chopped
1 red onion, finely chopped
3 tablespoons chopped flat-leaf parsley
1 tablespoon balsamic vinegar
2 tablespoons extra-virgin olive oil
salt & freshly ground black pepper

10

12-15   1   Heat the olive oil and butter in a roasting pan and fry the John Dory fillets, browning them on both sides. Add in the tomatoes, season and bake in a pre-heated oven at 220°C/425°F/Gas Mark 7 for about 8–10 minutes.

2-3   2   Meanwhile, prepare the salsa by mixing together all the ingredients.

4-5   3   Serve the fish with the softened tomato quarters, a spoonful of the salsa and a drizzle of extra-virgin olive oil, accompanied by lemon halves.

GRILLED TUNA STEAKS WITH A FENNEL, POTATO & TOMATO SALAD

Tuna are exceptionally fast swimmers as they need plenty of oxygen. When they swim at high speeds (up to 40 miles per hour) oxygenated water runs over their gills allowing them to breathe. All this swimming produces the powerful muscles which characterize tuna flesh. Serves 4.

30 minutes

salt & freshly ground black pepper
300 g/10 oz firkin or new potatoes
4–5 tablespoons extra-virgin olive oil
1 medium bulb of fennel, sliced
1 medium red onion, thinly sliced

1 tablespoon finely chopped flat-leaf parsley
juice of 1 lemon
1 tablespoon balsamic vinegar
4 plum tomatoes, cut into segments
4 x 200 g/7 oz tuna steaks

5

15   1   Bring a saucepan of salted water to the boil and cook the potatoes.

2-3   2   Meanwhile, heat 2 tablespoons of the oil in a frying pan, add the sliced fennel and stir-fry for a couple of minutes. Season and set aside. In a bowl mix together the onion, parsley, remaining oil, lemon juice and vinegar.

4   3   When the potatoes are cooked drain and refresh under cold running water for a couple of minutes, then while still warm quarter and toss in the prepared dressing with the fennel and tomatoes. Toss gently but thoroughly and set aside.

4-5   4   Heat a grilling pan and when it is hot, cook the seasoned tuna steaks to your preferred taste. Serve with the still warm salad and a little more extra-virgin olive oil, if necessary.

SEARED SALMON ESCALOPES ON A WATERCRESS, SUN-DRIED TOMATO & SPRING ONION SALAD WITH BASIL OIL

20 minutes

Salmon belongs to the northern hemisphere (Atlantic and Pacific oceans) and is one of its better known fish. Serves 4.

4 tablespoons extra-virgin olive oil
12–15 large basil leaves
salt & freshly ground black pepper
150 g/5 oz watercress, washed & drained
6 sun-dried tomatoes, cut into thin strips
4 spring onions, thinly sliced
4 x 200 g/7 oz salmon escalopes
2 lemons, halved

5

1   Blend the oil and basil with a pinch of salt in a liquidizer and set aside.

3

2   In a bowl toss together the watercress, sun-dried tomatoes, spring onions and a little of the basil oil.

1

3   Heat a dry, heavy-based frying pan until very hot, then sear the seasoned salmon escalopes for 3–4 minutes on each side if you like your salmon slightly rare in the middle, or a little longer to cook through.

6

4   Arrange the salad on individual serving plates, top with the salmon, sprinkle with the basil oil and serve with half a lemon.

1

BAKED SARDINES SERVED ON ROCKET LEAVES WITH AVOCADO & MARINATED RED ONION

Sardines are a favourite fish for many people. They are full of flavour and must be bought very fresh because, like all oily fish, the flesh spoils quickly. Serves 4.

30 minutes

1 tablespoon brown sugar
1 tablespoon balsamic vinegar
2–3 tablespoons red wine vinegar
salt & freshly ground black pepper
1 red onion, thinly sliced
12 sardines gutted, heads removed & well washed to remove all the scales
2 small avocados
150 g/5 oz rocket leaves, washed & drained

For the dressing
1 teaspoon mustard
3 tablespoons extra-virgin olive oil
1 tablespoon white wine vinegar
salt & freshly ground black pepper

5

22

1 First marinate the onion: in a bowl stir together the sugar, balsamic vinegar, red wine vinegar and a pinch of salt. When the salt and sugar have dissolved, add the onion. Toss well and leave to marinate for 20 minutes.

10

2 Place the sardines on a baking tray and season. Bake in a pre-heated oven at 220°C/425°F/Gas Mark 7 for about 10 minutes.

1

3 Make the dressing by blending the ingredients in a bowl with a fork. Set aside.

2-3

4 When the fish is ready, peel, stone and slice the avocados. Toss the rocket leaves with slices of avocado and the drained marinated onions. Place the salad on individual serving plates and arrange the fish on top. Sprinkle with the dressing and serve.

STUFFED SARDINES AIDA

The name of the dish does not refer to the famous opera, but to Aida Lavagna, a vivacious and talented cook, larger than life and twice as much fun. Dressed to kill and adored with her permanent, exotic turban, she used to make these delicious little snacks to be eaten cold on the plaza. Sadly Aida is no longer with us, but her memory lives on in this wonderfully simple dish. Serves 4.

25 minutes

12 sardines, butterflied with head and central bone removed (ask the fishmonger to do this for you)
100 g/4 oz ground almonds or bread crumbs
6 anchovy fillets, chopped
75 g/3 oz cheese, grated (strong-flavoured Spanish, or Cheddar will do)
1 tablespoon capers, chopped
3 tablespoons parsley or dill, finely chopped
a few sprigs of marjoram, finely chopped
grated zest and juice of ½ lemon
1 egg

5

salt & freshly ground black pepper

1

1 Heat the oven to maximum (250°C/475°F/Gas Mark 9).

(10-15)

2 To butterfly the sardines, first scale and wash them. Remove the heads and split the fish open. Grab hold of the spinal bone and slide a small knife along the bone, lifting it and separating it clean from flesh.

2

3 Mix the ground almonds together with the chopped anchovies and half the cheese. Reserve the other half of the cheese. Add the rest of the ingredients and mix well.

4 Lay 6 sardines, skin down, on a chopping board. Top each with about a tablespoon of the stuffing and spread to an even layer. Sandwich with the remaining 6 sardines. Transfer the sardine pairs to a well oiled baking dish, brush with olive oil and sprinkle with the rest of the cheese. Bake on the top shelf of the hot oven for 10-12 minutes until the sardines are cooked and nicely browned. Serve with wedge of lemon, on a bed of lettuce, either hot or at room temperature. The stuffed sardines can also be grilled or barbecued.

15-20

BAKED MACKEREL WITH CARROT NOODLES & ORANGE & CORIANDER DRESSING

This beautifully shiny fish has a high oil content which makes it ideal for grilling and baking. Serves 4.

20 minutes

4 large carrots
4 x 225 g/8 oz mackerel fillets
salt & freshly ground black pepper
1 teaspoon coriander seeds, crushed
2 shallots, finely diced
zest of 1 orange, grated
2 tablespoons fresh coriander leaves, finely chopped
1 tablespoon balsamic vinegar

5

2 tablespoons extra-virgin olive oil

4

1   Using a potato peeler, shave the carrots into 'noodles'.

2   Season the mackerel fillets with salt, pepper and the crushed coriander seeds. Place on a baking tray skin-side up and bake in a pre-heated oven at 230°C/450°F/Gas Mark 8 for 10 minutes.

12

3   Meanwhile, bring a saucepan of salted water to the boil and blanch the carrot noodles for a couple of seconds, then refresh under cold running water and drain well.

2

1

4   In a bowl mix together the shallots, orange zest, coriander leaves, vinegar, oil and seasoning.

5   When the fish is ready, arrange the noodles on a serving plate and season with a little of the dressing. Place the fish fillets on top, spoon over the remaining dressing and serve.

1

STUFFED MACKEREL

The mackerel, like the tuna, is loved all over the Mediterranean. Indeed freshly caught mackerel plainly barbecued on the quayside, served with a sharp sauce such as Agro-Dolce (see page ??) or just lemon juice, is one of the great pleasures of the Mediterranean summer.

This is an interpretation of an old Hebrew recipe. Serves 4.

30 minutes

4-6 small mackerel, cleaned & as fresh as possible
3 tablespoons lemon juice
100 g/4 oz dry white wine
small bunch of dill
salt & freshly ground black pepper
50 g/2 oz fish stock or water
500 g/1 lb leeks with some of the green left on, washed, trimmed & sliced

5

1   1   Heat the oven to 220°C/425°F/Gas Mark 7.

1   2   Make 3 deep slashes on each side of the fish and sprinkle both outside and inside with the lemon juice and salt. Allow to marinate until the stuffing is ready.

2-3   3   Place the leeks and dill in a food processor and process, starting and stopping the machine, until roughly chopped. Season with salt and pepper.

   4   Divide half of the leek mixture equally between the fish and stuff it into the cavity. Use the rest to line the bottom of a large, well greased, baking dish. Place the fish on the leek bed and pour the wine and stock over. Season and bake in the oven, uncovered, for about 15-20 minutes, turning the fish once and basting frequently. Serve either hot or cold accompanied by a salad such as celery and tomato (see page 92) or prawn and orange salad (see page 86) or Moroccan lemon salad (see page 96).

20-25

LIBYAN FISH

This is a delicious and extremely easy way of cooking oily fish such as grey mullet or mackerel. Here it is served hot but it is also good served as a part of a cold buffet. Serves 4.

30 minutes

3 tablespoons olive oil
1 teaspoon whole cumin seeds
1 small head of garlic, peeled & chopped
1-2 green chillies, sliced (optional)
juice of 1 lemon
150 ml/6 fl.oz fish stock or water
salt
1 kg/2 lb fish, cleaned & sliced into 6-8 portions
1 tablespoon capers, rinsed
a small bunch of flat-leaf parsley, leaves only

5

2-3

1 Heat the oil in a heavy-based frying pan, add the cumin and fry until the seeds start to pop and emit a pleasant, roasted smell.

7-8

2 Add the garlic and chillies if used and continue frying until the garlic starts to change colour. Add the lemon juice and stock, and bring to the boil. Reduce the heat and simmer for 5 minutes.

15-16

3 Add the fish, season with salt, cover and simmer for 15 minutes or until the fish is just done. Sprinkle with capers and parsley and serve, decorated with lemon wedges.

GRILLED PINK TROUT FILLET ON A HERB SALAD WITH MARINATED MUSHROOMS

20 minutes

Substitute the trout in the recipe with lemon sole fillets, brill or turbot for different contrasts of textures. Serves 4.

150 g/5 oz brown button mushrooms, stalks removed & finely sliced
1 red onion, finely diced
1 small clove of garlic, finely chopped
1 tablespoon chopped flat-leaf parsley
juice & rind of 1 lemon
salt & freshly ground black pepper
3 tablespoons extra-virgin olive oil
150 g/5 oz mixed lettuce leaves (preferably small ones)
6 chives, cut into 5 cm/2 in pieces
2 tablespoons chervil leaves
1 sprig of lemon thyme, leaves removed
2 tablespoons flat-leaf parsley leaves

10

4 x 170 g/6 oz pink trout fillets, skin removed

1

1 Place the mushrooms in a bowl with the onion, garlic, chopped parsley, lemon juice and rind. Season well and stir in the oil. Cover and leave to stand.

2

2 Toss the lettuce leaves with the herbs and set aside in a salad bowl.

6

3 Heat a grilling pan and when it is hot, sear the seasoned fish fillets for 2–3 minutes on each side (longer if you like your fish well done).

1

4 Arrange some salad on individual serving dishes, place the cooked fish on top and spoon on the marinated mushrooms. Buttered rice or new potatoes would make a suitable accompaniment.

Grilled Pink Trout Fillet on a Herb Salad with
Marinated Mushrooms, and Roasted Monkfish
with Grilled Courgettes & a Black Olive
& Pine-nut Relish (page 174)

ROASTED MONKFISH *with* GRILLED COURGETTES *& A* BLACK OLIVE *&* PINE-NUT RELISH

30 minutes

Monkfish is a seriously ugly fish with a head almost twice the size of its body. The skinned tails are the most commonly eaten part, and some fishmongers sell the cheeks as a delicacy. Serves 4.

4 tablespoons olive oil
4 x 225 g/8 oz monkfish tails, skinned
salt & freshly ground black pepper
3 medium courgettes, cut into thin diagonal slices
zest of 1 lemon, finely chopped
2 tablespoons extra-virgin olive oil
2 tablespoons flat-leaf parsley

For the relish
100 g/4 oz black olives, rinsed & well drained
100 g/4 oz pine-nuts, lightly roasted
1 clove of garlic
75 g/3 oz flat-leaf parsley leaves
juice of 1 lemon
3 tablespoons olive oil
salt & freshly ground black pepper

5

2   1   First make the relish by blending all the ingredients in a food processor. Check the seasoning and set aside.

22   2   Heat a couple of tablespoons of olive oil in a roasting pan and sear the monkfish. Season and cook in a pre-heated oven at 220°C/425°F/Gas Mark 7 for 15–20 minutes.

5   3   Meanwhile, heat a grilling pan and when it is hot, grill the courgette slices, a few at a time. As you cook them, toss them into a bowl with the lemon zest, oils, parsley and seasoning.

1   4   When the monkfish is ready, serve with a mound of marinated courgettes and a spoonful of relish.

POACHED FILLETS OF LEMON SOLE ON A RICE SALAD WITH ROASTED PEPPER SALSA

30 minutes

Rice and fish can be a wonderful combination. In this case the rice offers a contrasting texture to the fish and is a perfect foil for the salsa. Serves 4.

salt & freshly ground black pepper
200 g/7 oz basmati rice, washed
1 tablespoon small capers, rinsed & squeezed dry
3 tablespoons finely chopped chives
2 small plum tomatoes, de-seeded & finely chopped
3 tablespoons extra-virgin olive oil
50 g/2 oz unsalted butter
6 x 150 g/5 oz lemon sole fillets, halved lengthwise

For the salsa
2 medium red peppers
1 medium yellow pepper
½ red onion, thinly sliced
3 tablespoons extra-virgin olive oil
1 tablespoon balsamic vinegar
salt & freshly ground black pepper

10

15-20

1 Place the peppers on a baking tray and bake in a pre-heated oven at 240°C/450°F/Gas Mark 8 for 15–20 minutes, turning occasionally. Remove from the oven and leave to cool.

10-15

2 Meanwhile, bring a saucepan of salted water to the boil and cook the rice. When ready, drain and refresh under cold running water. Toss the rice into a bowl with the capers, chives, tomatoes, oil and seasoning. Mix well and set aside.

10-12

3 Place on the stove a frying pan with high sides and half fill it with water. Add the butter and some seasoning and bring to a simmer. Fold the sole fillets in half and poach in the liquid over a low heat for about 8–10 minutes.

5

4 Meanwhile, peel the peppers, cut into small dice and mix with the onion, oil, vinegar and seasoning.

2

5 When the fish is ready, spoon the rice on to a serving dish, arrange the fish fillets on top, spoon over the salsa and serve.

RED MULLET IN A PARCEL

Barbunya – or Sultan Ibrahim as it is known by the Arabs – is king of the Mediterranean fish. This small red relative of the Atlantic red mullet, with a golden stripe running along its body, is the embodiment of fishiness – it smells of sea and iodine and has an exquisite, white, flaky flesh. It is not surprisingly called the woodcock of the sea.

The best way to cook the fish is to dip it in seasoned flour and fry it crisply in boiling olive oil. In many countries the mullet is not gutted before cooking as the innards and especially the liver impart an intense gamey flavour.

The recipe below is almost as good. Mediterranean barbunya appears from time to time in many fishmongers and is well worth trying. If unobtainable use Atlantic red mullet. Serves 4.

30 minutes

6 pieces of silver foil measuring 20 x 20 cm/8 x 8 in
3 tablespoons olive oil
1 medium fennel, sliced across thinly
1 medium onion, sliced into thin rings
6 red mullets, scaled, cleaned & washed
a few sprigs of thyme
2 cloves of garlic, peeled & sliced thinly
6 thin slices of lemon
5 *salt & freshly ground black pepper*

1 1 Pre-heat the oven to 200°C/400°F/Gas Mark 6.

2 Oil the centre of each foil square generously (this will use roughly half the oil) and distribute the sliced fennel
2-3 and onion evenly.

3 Stuff the cavity of each fish with a sprig of thyme and some garlic and lay them on top of the vegetables. Sprinkle with the rest of the oil. Lay a slice of lemon on each, season with salt and pepper and parcel up tightly.
20 Bake them in the pre-heated oven for 10-15 minutes, opening the parcels for the last 5 minutes.

4 When the fish is nicely browned, serve decorated with lemon wedges. If more salt is needed, sprinkle with a bit
1 of coarse sea salt.

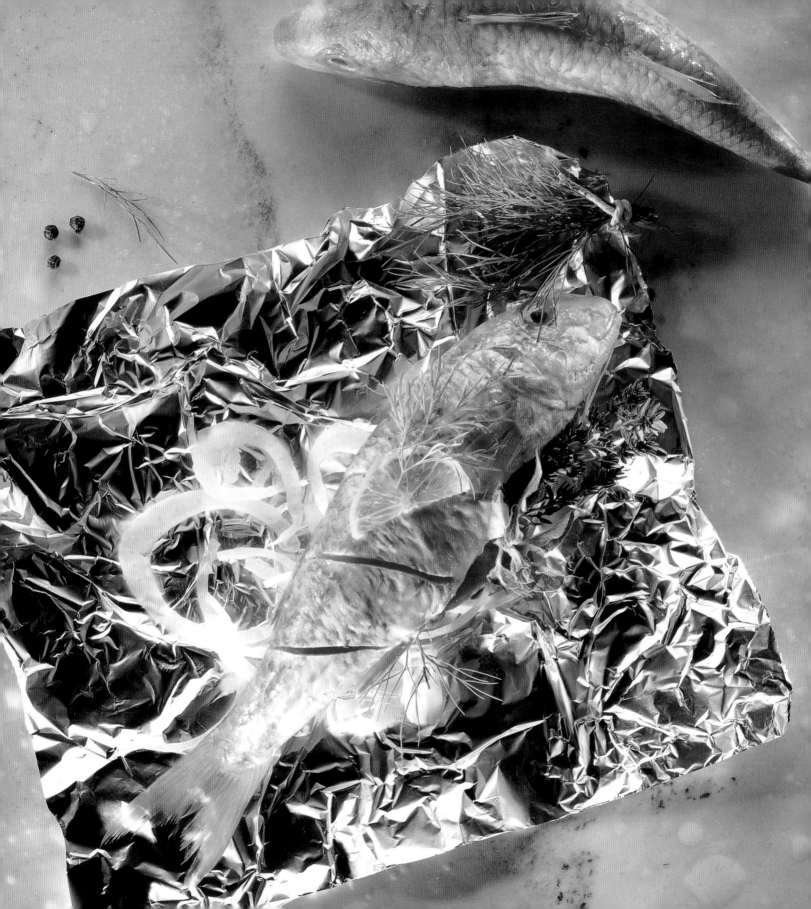

BAKED COD FILLETS WITH ROASTED LEEKS & HERB MAYONNAISE

Cod was once one of the most widely caught fishes, bought salted and dried. However, as the fishing grounds have been depleted fresh cod has become dearer and its culinary merits rediscovered. Serves 4.

25 minutes

4 tablespoons olive oil
25 g/1 oz unsalted butter
4 x 170 g/6 oz cod fillets
salt and freshly ground black pepper
75 g/3 oz plain flour
4 medium leeks, sliced & washed

For the mayonnaise
3 egg yolks
2 teaspoons Dijon mustard
1½ tablespoons white wine vinegar
400 ml/14 fl.oz olive oil
1 tablespoon finely chopped flat-leaf parsley
1 tablespoon finely chopped chives
1 tablespoon finely chopped dill
1 tablespoon chervil leaves
juice of 1 lemon
salt & freshly ground black pepper

5

3

1 Heat 1 tablespoon of the oil with the butter in a roasting pan. Dust the cod fillets with the seasoned flour, shaking off any excess. Fry the dusted fillets in the hot fat until golden on both sides.

2 Heat the remaining oil in a second roasting pan, add the leeks and cook over a high heat for a couple of minutes, then season. Cook the fish and leeks in a pre-heated oven at 220°C/425°F/Gas Mark 7 for about 10 minutes.

15

3 Meanwhile, prepare the mayonnaise: in a food processor blend together the egg yolks, mustard and vinegar, then add the oil in a steady stream, with the machine still running. When the mixture is well blended, spoon into a bowl and add the herbs, lemon juice and seasoning. Set aside.

3

1

4 When the fish and leeks are ready, arrange on serving plates and serve accompanied by the mayonnaise.

SAUTÉ OF SQUID, PRAWNS, MANGETOUT & BABY SWEETCORN WITH GARLIC & LEMON

Squid can be found in all the oceans and seas except the Black Sea. As far as cooking is concerned, it is most popular with oriental and Mediterranean cooks. Serves 4.

20 minutes

2 tablespoons olive oil
225 g/8 oz squid, cleaned, cut into strips & well drained
225 g/8 oz prawns, cooked & peeled
2 cloves of garlic, finely chopped
2 sun-dried tomatoes, cut into thin strips
150 g/5 oz mangetout, topped, tailed & cut in half
150 g/5 oz baby sweetcorn, quartered
juice & grated rind of 1 lemon
salt & freshly ground black pepper

10

1 tablespoon toasted sesame seeds

3

1 Heat the oil in a wok or large frying pan until it is almost smoking. Carefully toss in the squid and prawns and stir-fry for a couple of minutes.

3

2 Add the garlic, sun-dried tomatoes, mangetout and sweetcorn. Keep cooking over a high heat for a further 2 minutes, then add the lemon juice and rind.

1

3 Check the seasoning, sprinkle with sesame seeds and serve.

FISH COUSCOUS

On the Mediterranean coast of Africa couscous is more than a dish, it is a way of life. Couscous is a staple made from semolina coated with flour; when steamed those little grains are light and fluffy, the ideal medium for soaking the delicious gravy of soupy stews served with couscous. The stew can be made from practically anything: lamb, beef, game, poultry or fish. It should be cooked with plenty of vegetables and chickpeas making couscous a deliciously satisfying, well balanced and healthy meal.

Steaming couscous in the traditional way is a lengthy process. The following recipe, however, gives an easy and quick way for cooking it and, although the results are not quite as light and fluffy as the original, it does produce a very good alternative. Serves 6-8.

30+ minutes

for the couscous
5 tablespoons good olive oil
500 g/1 lb couscous
1 litre/2 pints stock or water
1 scant teaspoon salt

for the stew
3 tablespoons light olive oil or groundnut oil
1 teaspoon ground coriander seeds
½ teaspoon whole cumin seeds
½ cinnamon quill or scant ½ teaspoon powdered cinnamon
8 shallots, peeled & quartered
4 cloves of garlic, peeled & quartered
3 courgettes, trimmed & sliced
1 fennel bulb, sliced
1 litre/2 pints fish stock or ½ water and ½ dry white wine
a large pinch of saffron (optional)
salt
750 g/1½ lb steaky white fish such as halibut, monkfish & cod, a mixture, sliced into large chunks
1 tablespoon coriander, roughly chopped

5

½ recipe harissa (see page 257) so each diner can have a taste

1 To make the couscous, heat the oil in a heavy-based pan. Add the couscous and fry for a minute or two or until the grains start to change colour. Add the liquid and the salt and bring to the boil. Reduce the heat to a minimum, cover the pot tightly and simmer, very gently, for 20 minutes. Switch off the heat and let the couscous rest for about 5 minutes. Fluff up with a fork.

27-30

2 To make the stew, heat the oil in a large, heavy-based pan. Add the spices and fry for a second or two. Add the vegetables and continue frying, mixing until all the ingredients are shining and nicely coated with the spice mixture. Add the stock, wine and saffron, and bring to the boil. Reduce the heat to a minimum and simmer very gently for 10-15 minutes. Add the fish and continue to simmer for 8-10 minutes or until the fish is just tender when tested with the tip of a knife.

20-25

3 In a large flat serving bowl, arrange a crown of couscous. Lay the cooked fish and vegetables in the centre and pour some of the cooking liquid over the fish. Decorate with fresh coriander or parsley leaves and serve together with the rest of the cooking liquid and the harissa.

3

FISH COOKED IN A SPICY TOMATO SAUCE

This tasty and easy recipe comes from Tunis. The fish is first lightly fried and then cooked in spicy tomato sauce. Other fish suitable for this treatment include cod, salmon or tuna, but it is especially good with grey mullet. Serve the fish with rice, couscous or burgul and a chilled glass or two of dry white wine. Serves 4.

30+ minutes

Olive oil for shallow frying
75 g/3 oz flour
2 teaspoons sweet paprika
scant teaspoon salt
½ teaspoon freshly ground black pepper
4-6 fish steaks
½ bunch of flat-leaf parsley
½ quantity spicy tomato sauce (see page 269)
juice & grated zest of 1 lemon
5   *lemon wedges & chopped parsley for decoration*

1   Heat the oil in a heavy-based frying pan. Mix the flour with the seasoning and dust the fish well. Fry the steaks in the hot oil for a few minutes each side until the pieces are nicely golden. Lift out and drain on absorbent
8-10   paper.

2   Arrange the chopped parsley at the bottom of a large, heavy bottomed pan and arrange the fish on top. Add the tomato sauce, juice and grated zest of the lemon, mix well and pour over the fish. Bring to the boil, reduce the heat and simmer very gently for 15 minutes. Decorate with lemon wedges and parsley and serve either hot or at
20   room temperature.

GRILLED FISH SERVED WITH TARAMASALATA

This recipe was invented in a moment of desperation. Once on holiday, a friend arrived with a fresh catch and the refrigerator, except for a covered jar of home made tarama, was empty like an Arctic desert. Since then the dish has developed into a remarkably subtle combination of flavours and textures. Serves 4.

25 minutes

4-6 medium white-fleshed fish, each weighing about
    150 g/6 oz–250 g/8 oz, cleaned & washed well
3 tablespoons lemon juice
salt
5   *olive oil for brushing*

for the tarama (see page 79 & use half the quantity
    50 g/2 oz–75 g/3 oz yogurt, cream or milk
parsley and lemon wedges for decoration

1   1   Heat the grill to maximum.

2   Make 3 deep slashes on each side of the fish and sprinkle, both outside and inside, with lemon juice and salt. Arrange the fish in the grill pan, brush with oil and grill for 8-10 minutes. Turn the fish, brush with oil and
17-20   grill for a further 8-10 minutes or until the fish is ready.

2   3   For the sauce, dilute the tarama with the yogurt, cream or milk.

4   Pour a small ladle of the sauce on each plate. Place the fish on it and serve garnished with parsley leaves and
1   lemon wedges.

PRAWNS IN TOMATO & CHILLI SAUCE

This recipe was inspired by a classic Provençal dish. Use good quality raw prawns. You can peel them before cooking but the result will be a bit insipid. Serves 4.

25 minutes

3 tablespoons olive oil
½ teaspoon whole fennel seeds
100 g/4 oz shallots, peeled & chopped
3 cloves of garlic, peeled & roughly chopped
1-2 red or green chillies
2 bay leaves
2 strips of lemon zest

2 large, ripe beef tomatoes, peeled, de-seeded &
   roughly chopped
150 ml/6 fl.oz fish stock or dry white wine
500 g/1 lb raw prawns
salt & freshly ground black pepper
2 tablespoons chopped dill

5

9-10

1 Heat the oil in a heavy-based frying pan. Add the fennel seeds and fry for a minute or two or until the seeds start to pop. Add the shallots, garlic, chillies, bay leaves and lemon zest and fry over high heat for a minute or two. Add the tomatoes and stock, bring to the boil, reduce the heat and simmer for 5 minutes.

9-10

2 Increase the heat and add the prawns. Season and continue cooking, stirring frequently, for about 5-8 minutes or until the prawns are just done. Serve hot on a bed of rice, couscous or burgul, and sprinkle over the chopped dill.

BAKED SEA BASS

Sea bass is one of the most treasured fish of the Mediterranean. It has a delicate moist flesh which maintains its shape after cooking. This is one of the best and easiest ways of cooking sea bass.

Grated fresh ginger is not traditional in the Mediterranean kitchen, although in its dry form it is used extensively, appearing in savoury as well as sweet recipes. Serves 4.

30 minutes

1 large sea bass, weighing about 1½ kg/3 lb
3 tablespoons parsley, roughly chopped
1 tablespoon thyme, chopped
2 cloves of garlic, peeled & finely chopped
juice & grated zest of 1 lemon
2 teaspoons fresh ginger, grated
6 sprigs rosemary
5 tablespoons good olive oil
salt & freshly ground black pepper

5

1

1 Heat the oven to 230°C/450°F/Gas Mark 8.

2-3

2 Mix together the parsley, thyme, garlic, lemon zest and ginger. Stuff this mixture into the cavity of the fish.

2-3

3 Oil a shallow ovenproof dish and line it with the rosemary. Lay the fish on top. Mix the olive oil with the lemon juice and pour over the fish.

20-25

4 Bake in the oven, uncovered, for 20-25 minutes, basting from time to time. Serve hot, accompanied by Salsa Verde (see page 265).

VEGETARIAN

GRILLED BEEF TOMATOES WITH BLACK OLIVE, FETA CHEESE & CHIVE TOPPING

Feta is traditionally made with ewe's milk and sometimes goat's milk. It should be lightly salty in flavour and crumbly in texture. Serves 4.

25 minutes

> *225 g/8 oz feta cheese, grated*
> *100 g/4 oz black olives, washed, pitted & roughly chopped*
> *1 tablespoon finely chopped chives*
> *1 clove of garlic, finely chopped*
> *1 tablespoon dry breadcrumbs*
> *4 tablespoons extra-virgin olive oil*
> *salt & freshly ground black pepper*
> *4 large beef tomatoes, halved*
> *1 tablespoon olive oil*

5

> *100 g/4 oz rocket leaves, to serve*

2-3

1   In a bowl mix the feta with the olives, chives, garlic, breadcrumbs, 3 tablespoons of the extra-virgin olive oil and plenty of freshly ground black pepper. Sprinkle on to the cut side of the tomatoes, trying to cover the whole surface as neatly as possible.

12

2   Grease a baking tray with the olive oil and arrange the prepared tomatoes on it. Bake at 220°C/425°F/Gas Mark 7 for about 10 minutes until the topping is golden and the tomatoes heated through but still firm.

3

3   When the tomatoes are ready, serve on rocket leaves arranged on individual serving plates and drizzle over the remaining extra-virgin olive oil.

Grilled Beef Tomatoes with Black Olive,
Feta Cheese & Chive Topping,
and Baked Aubergines with Goat's
Cheese Mayonnaise (page 195)

ROAST VEGETABLES WITH TAHINA DRESSING

Tahina paste is obtained by crushing sesame seeds. It is delicious as a dip for raw or roast vegetables, as prepared in this recipe, but can also be served with plain grilled meat and fish. You can even try mixing it with the puréed flesh of roasted aubergines: a traditional Middle Eastern recipe. Serves 4.

25-30 minutes

4 tablespoons olive oil
1 bulb of fennel, cut into segments
2 red peppers, de-seeded & quartered
2 yellow peppers, de-seeded & quartered
1 red onion, cut into segments
1 leek, sliced
1 courgette, sliced
100 g/4 oz baby sweetcorn, halved
1 medium carrot, peeled & sliced
8 shitake mushrooms, stalks removed
4 plum tomatoes, halved
salt & freshly ground black pepper

For the tahina dressing
3 tablespoons tahina paste
½ tablespoon clear honey
50 ml/2 fl.oz extra-virgin olive oil
2 cloves of garlic, peeled
60 ml/3 fl.oz water
4–5 sprigs, flat-leaf parsley
salt & freshly ground black pepper
½ red chilli, de-seeded (optional)

5

1   Heat the oil in two baking trays. When hot, carefully toss in the vegetables and stir thoroughly. Season and roast in a pre-heated oven at 240°C/450°F/Gas Mark 8 for 10–15 minutes, stirring occasionally.

15-20

2   Meanwhile, prepare the dressing by blending all the ingredients in a liquidizer. Check the seasoning and set aside.

3

3   When the vegetables are ready, arrange on individual serving plates, drizzle over the dressing and serve. A crisp salad, rice or cous cous would make this a complete meal.

2

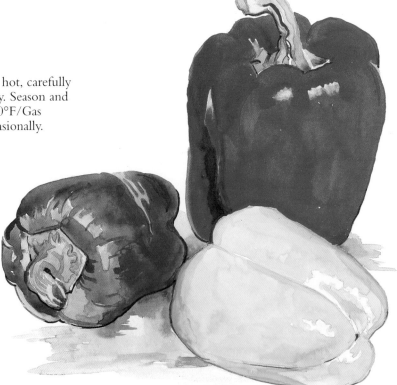

COURGETTE, RICOTTA & BASIL TIMBALE

For this recipe use aluminium dariole or timbale moulds as the heat will spread faster than if using glass or ceramic ramekins. Serves 4.

35 minutes

250 g/9 oz ricotta cheese
1 egg
3 tablespoons extra-virgin olive oil
3 courgettes, washed & grated
12–16 basil leaves, chopped
50 g/2 oz Parmesan cheese, grated
salt & freshly ground black pepper
4 tablespoons dry breadcrumbs
25 g/1 oz soft butter

For the salsa
6 plum tomatoes, quartered, de-seeded & diced
1 bunch of chives, finely chopped
1 tablespoon balsamic vinegar
3 tablespoons extra-virgin olive oil
salt & freshly ground black pepper

1　In a bowl whisk the ricotta with the egg and oil until well blended. Then fold in the courgettes, basil, Parmesan, seasoning and half the breadcrumbs.

2　Grease 4 individual dariole moulds with the butter and dust with the remaining breadcrumbs.

3　Spoon the mixture into the moulds. Place on a baking tray and cook in a pre-heated oven at 200°C/400°F/Gas Mark 6 for about 20 minutes.

4　Meanwhile, prepare the salsa by mixing together all the ingredients. Set aside..

5　When the timbales are ready, remove from the oven, unmould carefully on to individual serving plates and serve with the salsa.

POTATO RÖSTI SERVED WITH MUSHROOMS

Rösti is a thick potato pancake of Swiss origin which comes in many shapes and sizes. The potatoes are either coarsely grated or finely sliced and fried, usually raw, until soft in the middle with a crunchy, crisp crust on the outside. Rösti is served either with grated or melted cheese, soured cream, a savoury or sweet sauce or on its own.

Packaged rösti mix is now available in most large supermarkets, some even sell vacuum-packed, ready-made rösti which only needs heating. The mix makes a passable alternative if time is short.

Potatoes are notorious for absorbing oil and sticking to the bottom of a frying pan. To avoid this, use a non-stick pan. Serves 4.

35 minutes

1 kg/2¼ lb potatoes, peeled & coarsely grated
salt
50 g/2 oz butter or oil
2 eggs (size 3)
225 ml/8 fl. oz milk
freshly grated nutmeg

For the mushroom topping
2 tablespoons butter or oil
1 large onion, finely chopped
400 g/14 oz mushrooms, sliced
2 tablespoons soy sauce
salt & freshly ground black pepper
3 tablespoons mascarpone cheese
juice of ½ lemon

5

15-20

1 Sprinkle the grated potatoes with salt and mix well. Heat the butter or oil in a non-stick frying pan and add the grated potato, spreading it out into an even layer. Fry over a high heat for about 5 minutes, cover, reduce the heat to minimum and continue cooking for about 10 minutes until the potatoes are soft.

10

2 Beat the eggs together with the milk, flavour with nutmeg and pour over the potatoes in the pan. Cover and cook gently for about 10 minutes or until the egg is set. If the crust is ready and the top has not set, finish cooking under a hot grill.

11

3 Meanwhile, prepare the mushroom topping. Heat the butter or oil in a heavy-based frying pan, add the onion and fry over a high heat for 3–4 minutes until the onion is transparent. Add the mushrooms and soy sauce, and season with salt and pepper. Reduce the heat to medium and cook, uncovered, for about 6–8 minutes. Just before serving add the cheese and lemon juice and bring to the boil, mixing all the time. Switch off the heat.

2

4 To serve, turn the potato cake into a heated dish with the golden crust on top. Pour the mushrooms over and serve immediately.

POTATO, ONION & PEPPER RAGOÛT
WITH SAFFRON & MASCARPONE

30 minutes

Saffron is obtained by picking the stigmas of crocus flowers and drying them – a labour-intensive activity which accounts for the costliness of this wonderful spice. Serves 4.

50 g/2 oz unsalted butter
1 tablespoon olive oil
225 g/8 oz pearl onions, peeled
450 g/1 lb potatoes, peeled & cut into small cubes
1 clove of garlic, finely chopped
12 saffron strands

5

2 tablespoons dry white wine

1 tablespoon balsamic vinegar
2 red peppers, de-seeded & sliced
2 yellow peppers, de-seeded & sliced
225 g/8 oz mascarpone cheese
salt & freshly ground black pepper
2–3 tablespoons finely chopped flat-leaf parsley

1 Heat the butter and oil in a flameproof casserole. When they begin to foam, add the onions, potatoes, garlic and saffron strands. Fry for a few minutes, then add the wine and vinegar. Leave to evaporate for about a minute, then add the peppers and the mascarpone and mix well. Season.

6

10

2 Lower the heat, cover the casserole with a lid and simmer for 10 minutes.

3 Remove the lid, turn up the heat and cook for a further 5–8 minutes, stirring from time to time, until the juices are thick and creamy. Fold in the parsley and serve with cous cous or rice.

5-8

STIR-FRY OF CABBAGES WITH INDONESIAN NOODLES & PEANUTS

20 minutes

Oil noodles can be found already cooked in most Asian supermarkets. If you cannot find them, use dry Chinese noodles which are sold in most supermarkets. Serves 4.

3 tablespoons olive oil
100 g/4 oz red cabbage, thinly sliced
100 g/4 oz savoy cabbage, thinly sliced
100 g/4 oz pak choy, thinly sliced
3 anchovy fillets (optional)
1 clove of garlic, finely chopped
1 medium red onion, thinly sliced

10

1 red pepper, de-seeded & thinly sliced

450 g/1 lb Indonesian oil noodles
100 g/4 oz Chinese cabbage, thinly sliced
1 small red chilli, de-seeded & finely chopped
  (optional)
2 tablespoons ketjap manis (see page 158)
salt & freshly ground black pepper
150 g/5 oz peanuts, toasted & roughly chopped

1 Heat the oil in a wok or large frying pan until smoking. Carefully toss in the red cabbage, savoy cabbage, the sliced stalks of the pak choy, the anchovies, if used, and the garlic and stir-fry for a minute or two. Then add the onion and red pepper and stir-fry for a further couple of minutes.

5

2 Lastly add the noodles, Chinese cabbage, leaves of the pak choy, chilli and ketjap manis. Toss for a further minute or two until the noodles are heated through, check the seasoning and serve sprinkled with the peanuts.

3

NOTE: When stir-frying don't be tempted to add more oil if the ingredients seem too dry. Instead, add 1 tablespoon of water which will quickly evaporate: the steam produced will help cook the ingredients without burning them.

VEGETABLE TOAD-IN-THE-HOLE

Toad-in-the-hole conjures up images of sausages and meat, but this is not necessarily so. The following recipe gives an interesting, filling and delicious vegetarian alternative. Basically any favourite vegetable combination can go into the dish, the only stipulation being that the vegetables will cook in 20 minutes.

Ale or beer is not usually used for toad-in-the-hole batter but a good, malty, real ale adds an especially delicious nuttiness to the dish.

40+ minutes

Serve very hot with a vegetarian gravy, if liked, or on its own with a fresh salad. Serves 4.

4 tablespoons peanut oil
6 medium open mushrooms
6 small tomatoes
225 g/8 oz mature Cheddar cheese, cut into 6 chunks

For the batter
4 eggs (size 3), separated
225 ml/8 fl.oz ale, milk or water
225 g/8 oz plain flour
salt & freshly ground black pepper
a few sprigs of fresh thyme, finely chopped
1 tablespoon finely chopped fresh parsley
a few drops of tabasco
freshly grated nutmeg

2

1   1   Heat the oven to 200°C/400°F/Gas Mark 6.

5   2   First make the batter: whisk the egg whites until stiff. Beat the yolks together with the ale, milk or water.

3   Sift the flour into a large mixing bowl, season with salt and pepper and gradually add the liquid, herbs, tabasco and nutmeg to make a
8-10   smooth, thick batter. Fold in the whisked egg whites.

4   Heat the oil in a baking dish or tin until just smoking and add the batter. Arrange the vegetables and cheese in the batter and bake for about 20 minutes or until well-risen and golden-brown.
23-25   Serve very hot with Raw Beetroot and Apple Salad (see page 94).

PUMPKIN PILAFF

Pumpkins and gourds begin to appear in the market from the middle of September and are available until Christmas. Their variety is immense and they are mostly interchangeable in cooking.

Pumpkins are cheap and versatile. They can be made into chutneys, jams, pies, soups and fritters. When boiled, pumpkin absorbs a large amount of water and becomes mushy, therefore avoid boiling if possible – either steam, bake or fry.

This recipe is of Persian origin and uses burgul instead of rice. Burgul is probably the most ancient convenience food. It is actually made of pre-cooked and dried wheat, though it is misleadingly known as cracked wheat. Although it is cooked in this recipe, it can be used uncooked: simply soak the dried burgul in boiling water for about 20–25 minutes and drain well. Add a spoonful or two of good olive oil, reheat and serve instead of rice with your favourite sauce, or add cold burgul to salads. Serves 4.

35 minutes

150 g/5 oz coarse burgul, washed in a colander under running water
½ teaspoon saffron strands
225 ml/8 fl.oz vegetable stock
75 ml/3 fl.oz olive oil
1 onion, chopped
350 g/12 oz firm pumpkin or gourd, peeled & cubed
1 bouquet garni, made from 1 small cinnamon stick, 2 bay leaves
    & a strip or two of lemon or orange zest
salt & freshly ground black pepper
100 g/4 oz cashew nuts
1 tablespoon olive oil

5

3   1 Wash the burgul and cover with boiling water.

2   2 Soak the saffron in the stock.

3 Heat the oil in a heavy-based saucepan. Add the onion and fry for 1 minute, then add the pumpkin and fry over a high heat for a few minutes until the onion and pumpkin begin to take colour. Drain the burgul and add to the pumpkin mixture with the stock and saffron, the bouquet garni, salt and pepper and bring to the boil.

25-27   Reduce the heat and simmer very slowly for 15–20 minutes or until most of the liquid has evaporated.

3-5   4 Meanwhile, fry the cashew nuts in the tablespoon of oil until golden, then drain.

5 When the pilaff is ready, remove the bouquet garni, fold in the nuts, sprinkle with dill or mint and serve hot,
1   together with Orange and Olive Salad (see page 98).

BAKED FIELD MUSHROOMS *with* RICOTTA, PINE-NUTS & BASIL FILLING

Flat field mushrooms are commonly seen as the poor relation of wild mushrooms, probably because they are so easy to grow. If you know where to pick or buy wild flat field mushrooms make use of them instead. Serves 4.

30 minutes

250 g/9 oz ricotta cheese
2 tablespoons extra-virgin olive oil
75 g/3 oz pine-nuts, toasted
1 small clove of garlic, finely chopped
12 large basil leaves, chopped
salt & freshly ground black pepper
12 medium flat field mushrooms, stalks removed
1 tablespoon olive oil

For the dressing
2 plum tomatoes, quartered, de-seeded & diced
½ red onion, diced
1 tablespoon balsamic vinegar
salt & freshly ground black pepper

5

1 In a bowl mix the ricotta with half the extra-virgin olive oil, the pine-nuts, garlic, basil and seasoning. (The mixture should be moist and creamy; add 1–2 tablespoons of cream if necessary.)

1-2

2 Spoon the mixture on to the dark gills side of the mushrooms, pressing lightly to make it stick.

1

3 Grease a baking tray with the olive oil and arrange the stuffed mushrooms on it. Bake in a pre-heated oven at 220°C/425°F/Gas Mark 7 for about 15 minutes or until the mushrooms are soft through to the middle.

17

4 Meanwhile, prepare a dressing by mixing the tomatoes in a bowl with the onion, the remaining extra-virgin olive oil, the vinegar and seasoning.

3

5 When the mushrooms are ready, arrange on individual serving plates and serve with the dressing.

3

FENNEL, SUN-DRIED TOMATO, GOAT'S CHEESE & PINE-NUT GRATIN

Fennel is a delicious vegetable: serve it raw, thinly sliced in salad; steamed drizzled with extra-virgin olive oil, balsamic vinegar and Parmesan shavings; or braised with a little white wine for serving with fish, chicken or veal. It has good digestive properties. Serves 4.

30 minutes

salt & freshly ground black pepper
4 medium bulbs of fennel, cut into thin segments
25 g/1 oz soft unsalted butter

5

75 g/3 oz pine-nuts, lightly toasted

8 sun-dried tomatoes, cut into thin strips
1 bunch of chives, finely chopped
325 g/11 oz fresh goat's cheese, crumbled

4

1   Bring a saucepan of salted water to the boil and blanch the fennel for 1 minute, then drain well.

1

2   Grease an ovenproof dish (or 4 individual ones) with the soft butter and arrange the fennel in it. Sprinkle on some pine-nuts, some sun-dried tomatoes, some chives and some of the goat's cheese. Season.

3   Repeat the operation until all the ingredients are used up (no more than 3 layers). Then bake in a pre-heated oven at 220°C/425°F/Gas Mark 7 for about 15 minutes or until the cheese topping is melted and crisp. Serve

20

hot with a crisp salad and ripe tomatoes.

BAKED AUBERGINES WITH GOAT'S CHEESE MAYONNAISE

Aubergines are now a favourite vegetable but they haven't always been popular – they were once said to cause indecent behaviour in men and even be responsible for signs of madness! Luckily we have grown wiser as far as this extremely versatile vegetable is concerned. Serves 4.

30+ minutes

2 large aubergines
salt & freshly ground black pepper
4 tablespoons olive oil
2–3 whole cloves of garlic, lightly crushed
150 g/5 oz mixed salad leaves, washed & drained

For the mayonnaise
150 g/5 oz fresh goat's cheese, cold, crumbled
1 tablespoon wholegrain mustard
1 tablespoon white wine vinegar
1 tablespoon olive oil
2 tablespoons extra-virgin olive oil
grated rind & juice of ½ lemon
1 bunch of chives, finely chopped

5

1   Cut the aubergines in half lengthways, then crossways into segments. Sprinkle generously with salt and leave to drain for 20 minutes. Wash to remove the salt and pat dry.

22

2   Divide the oil between 2 roasting pans and heat until almost smoking, then very carefully toss in the aubergine and garlic. Bake in a pre-heated oven at 220°C/425°F/Gas Mark 7 for 15–20 minutes, tossing occasionally, until the aubergines are golden and soft through.

17-20

3   Meanwhile, make the mayonnaise: place the goat's cheese, mustard and vinegar in a food processor and whizz until well amalgamated, then pour in both the oils in a steady stream with the machine still running. Remove the mayonnaise from the food processor and stir in the lemon rind and juice, chives and seasoning. Mix well and chill until ready to use.

3

4   When the aubergines are ready remove from the oven and arrange on the prepared salad leaves, on individual serving plates, discarding the garlic. Season with freshly ground black pepper and spoon on the mayonnaise.

1

LEEK CLAFOUTIS

Clafoutis is the name of an ancient Gallic sweet, usually made with cherries, which is very similar to a fruit toad-in-the-hole. The fruit is added to a light batter flavoured with Armagnac and baked in the oven.

Modern chefs call anything that is embedded in a batter and baked 'clafoutis'. A version of this dish appeared in *Marie Claire*'s 'Cuisine Extraordinaire'. Somehow the Gallic word 'clafoutis' suits the Welsh leek perfectly, but cauliflower, broccoli, carrots or asparagus can be used with equal success. Serves 4.

30 minutes

750 g/1½ lb slender young leeks, trimmed & washed
salt & freshly ground black pepper
350 g/12 oz fromage frais
2 eggs (size 3), beaten
75 g/3 oz Roquefort or Stilton cheese, grated or crumbled
1 tablespoon chopped fresh flat-leaf parsley
butter for greasing

5
2 tablespoons hazelnut oil

1
1 Heat the oven to 225°C/425°F/Gas Mark 7.

10-12
2 Cook the leeks in plenty of boiling salted water for 10–12 minutes, then drain well. Or steam for 10 minutes. Meanwhile, mix the fromage frais with the eggs, half the cheese, salt, pepper and parsley.

2
3 Butter an ovenproof dish and mask with half the egg and cheese mixture. Lay the well-drained leeks on top and cover with the remaining sauce. Dot with the remaining cheese and sprinkle with the oil.

15
4 Bake in the pre-heated oven for 15 minutes. Serve either hot or at room temperature, accompanied by a fresh salad and a glass of chilled dry white wine such as Muscadet.

STUFFED SQUASH

Recently a wide range of squash has begun to appear on shelves of big supermarkets. They come in many shapes and sizes. They are easily handled, keep well and when unpeeled can be baked or steamed: having a hollow centre, they are ideal for stuffing. Peeled squash can also be fried but avoid boiling sliced squash as it becomes soggy very quickly. In most varieties the peel is too tough to eat but in some, especially small pattipans, it can be eaten.

For this dish use either small custard marrow, small gem squash or small round courgettes. Or slice a firm marrow into 5 cm/2 in slices and make a round hollow in each slice. Serves 4.

35-40 minutes

3 medium or 6 small gem squash
4–5 tablespoons good olive oil
1 large onion, peeled & quartered
1 red pepper, de-seeded & sliced
4 plum tomatoes, peeled, de-seeded & chopped
150 g/6 oz mature Cheddar or feta cheese, coarsely grated or crumbled
200 g/7 oz fresh wholemeal or white breadcrumbs
75 g/3 oz pine-nuts, dry-roasted until light brown
salt & freshly ground black pepper
4 tablespoons finely chopped fresh flat-leaf parsley or mint, or both

10

½ quantity Yogurt Tartar (see page 259) or Tahina Sauce (see page 257), to serve

1

1 Heat the oven to 230°C/450°F/Gas Mark 8.

10-12

2 Slice the squash into halves. With a spoon, remove the seeds and fibres, creating a fair-sized hollow deep enough for the stuffing. Steam the squash for 8–10 minutes or until just soft.

6-8

3 Meanwhile, make the stuffing. Gently heat the oil in a heavy-based frying pan. Put the onion and red pepper into a food processor and process at high speed, starting and stopping the machine until the vegetables are finely chopped but not puréed. Add to the heated oil and fry over a gentle heat for 3–4 minutes or until the onions begin to become transparent. Switch off the heat and add all the remaining ingredients. Mix well.

15-20

4 Pile the stuffing into the hollows in the squash, drizzle with some olive oil and bake for 10–12 minutes until hot and the top begins to brown. Top each with a good tablespoon of Yogurt Tartar and serve hot, accompanied by a fresh salad.

STEAMED BROCCOLI FLORETS ON GRILLED POLENTA WITH DOLCELATTE SAUCE

Polenta, as we know it, was first cooked in the Veneto region of Italy. The ships coming from the Americas unloaded their cargoes, which included maize, in Venice and the popularity of this ingredient quickly spread throughout northern Italy. Serves 4.

30 minutes

200 g/7 oz dolcelatte cheese, cut into small chunks
150 g/5 oz mascarpone cheese
1 tablespoon balsamic vinegar
2 tablespoons dry white wine
salt & freshly ground black pepper
700 g/1½ lb broccoli florets
2 spring onions, thinly sliced

For the polenta
500 ml/19 fl.oz water
500 ml/19 fl.oz milk
*2 tablespoons extra-virgin olive oil & a little extra for
    oiling*
1 clove of garlic, finely chopped
salt & freshly ground black pepper
250 g/9 oz instant polenta
50 g/2 oz pecan nuts, toasted & finely chopped

5

1 First make the polenta by bringing the water, milk, oil, garlic and seasoning to the boil in a saucepan. Pour in the polenta in a steady stream, stirring continuously. Cook for 5 minutes over a low heat, add the pecan nuts and stir well. Remove from the heat and spread on a lightly oiled baking tray. Leave to set in a cool place for about 20 minutes.

25

4-5

2 Place the dolcelatte, mascarpone, vinegar, white wine and seasoning in a saucepan and heat gently until melted.

4-5

3 Meanwhile, bring a saucepan of salted water to the boil and heat a grilling pan. When the water boils, cook the broccoli for a couple of minutes (longer if you prefer your vegetables less crunchy), then drain and keep warm.

2-3

4 Cut the polenta into quarters and grill for a couple of minutes on both sides.

1

5 Place the grilled polenta on individual serving plates, arrange the broccoli on top and spoon over the sauce. Sprinkle with the spring onion and freshly ground black pepper.

SPINACH, OYSTER MUSHROOM & TOMATO BRUSCHETTA
WITH PARMESAN SHAVINGS & TRUFFLE OIL

Bruschetta is essentially a slice of toasted or grilled bread rubbed with a fresh clove of garlic and drizzled with extra-virgin olive oil. You can then embellish it with tomato, basil, anchovies, ricotta, or whatever you wish. Serves 4.

15 minutes

2 tablespoons olive oil
50 g/2 oz unsalted butter
400 g/14 oz oyster mushrooms, stalks removed
1 clove of garlic, finely chopped
450 g/1 lb spinach, washed, drained & roughly chopped
2 plum tomatoes, cut into segments
salt & freshly ground black pepper
100 g/4 oz Parmesan cheese
2 tablespoons truffle oil

For the bruschetta
1 loaf of ciabatta bread, sliced
1 clove of garlic, halved

5

2-3

1 Make the bruschetta by toasting the ciabatta bread slices and then rubbing them while still hot with the garlic clove. Arrange on individual serving plates.

2 Heat the olive oil with the butter in a large frying pan until foaming, then add the mushrooms and garlic and fry briskly until the juices in the pan are clear. Quickly add the spinach and allow to wilt, then fold in the tomatoes. Check the seasoning, then pile on to the bruschetta.

4-5

3 Using a potato peeler, shave the Parmesan on to the spinach and mushroom mixture, drizzle on the truffle oil and enjoy.

2

SHAKSHUKA

A North African cousin of Provençal ratatouille, shakshuka is a mixture of vegetables fried in olive oil with the addition of herbs and spices: indeed, the name of the dish comes from the Moroccan word 'shachshucha' – a mixture. Many combinations of vegetables are used according to season and locality. What seems to be common to all versions is the use of tomatoes and peppers. Topped with an egg and served accompanied with Fennel and Grapefruit Salad (see page 94), it makes a delicious and surprisingly substantial summer main course.

The following recipe uses apples, which are not strictly authentic but add an interesting note of sweetness to the dish. Serves 4.

30 minutes

4 tablespoons olive oil
2 medium onions, chopped
3–4 cloves of garlic, chopped
1–2 chillies, chopped (optional)
2 sticks of celery, leaves included, chopped
300 g / 10 oz plum tomatoes, peeled & coarsely chopped
2 green peppers, de-seeded & sliced into rings
2 red peppers, de-seeded & sliced into rings
2 apples, cored & cubed
4 tablespoons chopped fresh coriander
salt

5

6 eggs (size 3)

1   Heat the oil in a large, heavy-based frying pan. Add the onion, garlic and chilli and fry over a high heat for about 5 minutes or until the mixture begins to brown. Add all the remaining ingredients except the eggs, reduce the heat and cook for about 15 minutes until the vegetables are cooked but still *al dente*. Stir from time to time and add a few tablespoons of stock or water if too dry.

20

2   When almost ready, break the eggs over the vegetables in the pan, cover and continue cooking for about 3–5 minutes until the whites are just set and the yolks still runny. Serve either hot or at room temperature with chunks of crisp French bread and a green salad.

3-5

CURRIED PINEAPPLE

Ready-peeled pineapples are becoming more widely available. They are usually sold in chilling cabinets, in units of 500 g/1 lb 2 oz. Although they tend to be on the under-ripe side they are perfectly suitable for cooking and save the messy process of peeling the fruit. This delicious and light curry goes surprisingly well with red wine such as shiraz or a very full-bodied chardonnay. Serves 4.

40 minutes

2 large onions, chopped
4 cloves of garlic
2.5 cm/1 in piece of fresh ginger, peeled
225 g/8 oz carrot, peeled
4 tablespoons peanut oil
1 tablespoon mustard seeds
1 fresh red chilli, chopped or ½ teaspoon chilli
*   powder or more to taste*
seeds of 5 cardamom pods
1 small cinnamon stick, broken
½ teaspoon ground turmeric
4 tablespoons cider or white wine vinegar
400 ml/14 fl.oz hot vegetable stock or water
1 tablespoon clear honey or brown sugar
salt
750 g/1 lb 10 oz fresh pineapple, peeled, cored &
*   cut into 4 cm/1½ in chunks*
75 g/3 oz flaked almonds
2 tablespoons chopped fresh coriander, to garnish

10

2-3

1   In a food processor process the onion, garlic, ginger and carrot until almost puréed.

2   Heat the oil in a heavy-based saucepan. Add the mustard seeds, chilli, if used, and spices and fry until the mustard seeds start to pop and emit a pleasant roasted aroma. Add the onion mixture and continue frying, over a high heat, for 5–6 minutes or until the mixture starts to take colour. Add the vinegar, the hot stock or water, honey or sugar and salt and bring to the boil. Reduce the heat and simmer, uncovered, for 12 minutes.

20

3   When the sauce is slightly thickened add the pineapple, mix well and simmer gently for about 3–5 minutes or until the pineapple is hot. Garnish with flaked almonds browned in a little oil and sprinkle with coriander. Serve with rice, burgul or noodles, accompanied by a fresh salad.

7

DRIED FRUIT PILAFF

The origin of this fragrant dish lies in the mountains of Kurdistan where it is cooked for special occasions. It is a delicious combination of fruit and either rice or burgul. It can be served very simply accompanied with yogurt to which chopped mint is added. Either serve it with a salad as a light supper dish or to accompany main dishes.

Use a combination of dried fruit such as raisins, sultanas, dried apricots, peaches and dried cherries. I sometimes also add dried mango or prunes. As they are cooked in the recipe the dried fruits do not need long pre-soaking, but it is advisable to soak them briefly in boiling water, especially if they are very dry. The quantity below is enough for 6 substantial portions as a main course or 8–10 as a side dish.

35 minutes

3 tablespoons olive oil
1 large onion, coarsely chopped
6 cardamom pods, broken
1 stick of cinnamon
½ scant teaspoon ground turmeric
2–3 bay leaves
2 dried lemons, broken into small pieces (optional)
400 g/14 oz rice or burgul
150 g/6 oz red lentils
225 g/8 oz mixed dried fruit
stock or water
salt & freshly ground black pepper
2–3 tablespoons finely chopped fresh mint or dill, to serve
about 300 g/10 oz plain yogurt, to serve

5

5-7

1 Heat the oil in a large heavy-based saucepan and add the onion, cardamom, cinnamon, turmeric, bay leaves and lemons, if used. Fry over a high heat for a few minutes until the onion begins to take colour.

2 Add all the remaining ingredients except the yogurt and mint, pouring in enough stock to cover the rice by about 1 cm/½ in. Season with salt and pepper, bring to the boil and reduce the heat to low. Cover the pan and simmer for about 20 minutes or until most of the liquid has evaporated. Check after 15 minutes and if too dry add a few more spoons of stock or water.

25

1

3 Mix the yogurt with the chopped mint and serve with the hot pilaff.

NOTE: Dried lemons, which are very aromatic, can be obtained from many continental and oriental food shops.

VEGETABLE CUTLETS SERVED WITH WALNUT TARATOR

Those light, herby and delicious fritters are ideal for a summer meal. Even before the recent advance of vegetarian cooking this versatile dish was common in many households. Unfortunately it was all too often abused, featuring tired, boiled vegetables and, not surprisingly, the results were disappointing, unfairly earning the dish a bad name.

When using carefully prepared, fresh ingredients the results are entirely different. The following combination is an excellent basic mixture but may be varied according to season and mood. Try making the cutlets with a mixture of celery and celeriac or carrot, coriander and parsnip: they are all delicious.

The cutlets can also be served with Fresh Tomato Sauce (see page 267) or Yogurt Tartar (see page 259). Serves 4.

20 minutes

1 bunch fresh flat-leaf parsley, tough stems removed
1 bunch fresh mint, tough stems removed
1 bunch spring onions, trimmed but green leaves included
500 g / 1 lb 2 oz courgettes, coarsely grated
2 carrots, peeled & coarsely grated
150 g / 5 oz mature Cheddar or any other well-matured hard cheese
6–8 tablespoons dry breadcrumbs or matzo meal
salt & freshly ground black pepper
oil, for shallow frying

5

½ quantity Walnut Tarator (see page 258)

3-5

1 Mince or process the herbs and spring onions. Transfer to a large mixing bowl and add all the remaining ingredients and mix well. If the mixture is too soft, add more breadcrumbs.

8-10

2 Heat the oil in a large, heavy-based frying pan and fry spoonfuls of the mixture for 4–5 minutes on each side or until golden-brown.

3

3 Drain well on kitchen paper and serve hot, accompanied by the Walnut Tarator. Serve with a burgul or rice pilaff and a fresh, herby green salad.

MIXED VEGETABLE CURRY

One of the most distinctive flavourings in this curry is the tamarind, the sour pulp which surrounds the seeds of the tamarind tree. It is sold in most Indian and oriental stores, either as a compressed slab or as a paste. The paste is the easiest to use as in the other form the tamarind needs to be soaked in hot water and sieved to get rid of the seed. Although lemon juice or vinegar can be used instead, they lack the distinct, fruity and surprisingly fresh flavour of the tamarind. Curry leaves are available from Indian grocers. Serves 4.

40 minutes

2 medium onions, unpeeled & halved
4 tablespoons peanut oil
1 scant tablespoon sesame seeds
1 tablespoon ground coriander
2 teaspoons cumin seeds
8 curry leaves
1/2 teaspoon ground turmeric
1 tablespoon tamarind paste
1 tablespoon clear honey or brown sugar
225 ml/8 fl.oz hot stock
salt
1/2 teaspoon chilli powder (optional)
100 g/4 oz baby sweetcorn, washed
100 g/4 oz courgettes, washed, trimmed & cut into chunks
1 very small savoy cabbage, cut into chunks
2 sweet red peppers, de-seeded & thickly sliced
150 g/6 oz broad beans, trimmed & sliced
3 small tomatoes, cut into large chunks
2 tablespoons chopped fresh flat-leaf parsley or coriander, to garnish

4

1 Heat the grill to medium. Lay the onion halves, cut sides down, on the grill rack and grill until the skins are charred (about 5 minutes). Peel off the skins and purée the onion in a food processor at high speed.

10

2 Heat the oil in a heavy-based saucepan. Add the sesame seeds, coriander, cumin, curry leaves and turmeric and fry over a high heat until a pleasant spicy aroma is emitted. Add the puréed onion and continue to fry for a few minutes.

10

3 Dissolve the tamarind paste and honey or sugar in the hot stock and add to the pan. Season with salt and add the chilli powder, if used. Bring to the boil and boil rapidly for 3–4 minutes. Add all the vegetables except the tomatoes, reduce the heat and cook, uncovered, for 8–10 minutes until the vegetables are cooked but still crunchy. Add the tomatoes, mix in and allow to heat through.

15

1

4 Garnish with parsley or coriander and serve hot, with rice or burgul, accompanied by a fresh salad.

VEGETABLE STEW WITH SEMOLINA DUMPLINGS

A substantial winter or autumn stew – a meal in itself – which warms the bones and fills hungry stomachs. The origin of the stew is the Middle East, but the topping is pure European. The combination of vegetables used is just one of a number of possibilities. Swedes, turnips, celeriac or any other vegetable in season can be added to give a different texture and flavour to the basic stew. Although the okra is optional, do try to use it as it thickens the sauce. Serves 4.

35 minutes

4 tablespoons strong Greek olive oil
1 large onion, coarsely chopped
4 cloves of garlic
2 medium carrots, peeled & coarsely chopped
3 sticks of celery, coarsely chopped
100 g/4 oz okra, trimmed & cut into short lengths (optional)
1 medium aubergine, unpeeled & cut into 2.5 cm/1 in cubes
150 g/5 oz courgettes, cut into small chunks
150 g/5 oz fresh broad beans or peas
300 g/10 oz beef or plum tomatoes, roughly chopped
225 ml/8 fl.oz hot vegetable stock
1 bouquet garni, made of a few sprigs of thyme, marjoram & a strip of lemon zest

For the dumplings
225 g/8 oz strong Cheddar cheese, grated
3 eggs (size 3)
75 g/3 oz semolina
3 tablespoons self-raising flour
2 tablespoons chopped fresh mixed herbs such as flat-leaf parsley, thyme, sage & marjoram
1 teaspoon grated lemon rind
salt & freshly ground black pepper
a handful of chopped fresh parsley, to garnish

10

1

1 Heat the oil in a heavy-based saucepan or flameproof casserole.

2 Put the onion, garlic, carrot and celery into a food processor and process at high speed, switching the machine on and off until the vegetables are finely chopped but not puréed. Add to the hot oil together with the remaining ingredients. Bring to the boil, then simmer gently for 8–10 minutes.

10-12

3 Meanwhile, make the dumplings by mixing all the ingredients together. Shape into about 6 x 5 cm/2 in patties and place over the top of the stew. Cover and cook for a further 10–15 minutes. Sprinkle with chopped parsley and serve piping hot.

15-20

NUT KOFTAS SERVED WITH YOGURT SAUCE

Those spicy, filling nut rissoles are a welcome change from the traditional nut cutlet. Their texture is light, moist and sweetish. The dish is based on a Jewish Moroccan recipe for a nut stuffing. Originally meat was used as a binder but the results are better without it, making the rissoles lighter, more moist and less fatty.

In the original recipe a large amount of sugar is used to sweeten the dish. In fact, this is unnecessary, especially when using pecan nuts, which are naturally sweet.

Any nuts can be used for the mixture. It is especially tasty as a combination of pecans and hazelnuts but almonds and peanuts are also excellent. For a fuller nut flavour, lightly roast the nuts first.

To make the dish even more calorie-conscious, instead of frying the rissoles arrange them raw in a greased baking dish. Pour the Yogurt Tartar over and bake in the oven pre-heated to 200°C/400°F/Gas Mark 6 for 35–40 minutes. Serves 4.

20 minutes

> *400 g / 14 oz nuts, lightly roasted*
> *2 tablespoons walnut oil*
> *2 eggs (size 3), beaten*
> *6 tablespoons fresh breadcrumbs or matzo meal*
> *1 tablespoon sugar (optional)*
> *1 teaspoon cinnamon*
> *1 teaspoon mace*
> *½ teaspoon ground ginger*
> *¼ teaspoon freshly grated nutmeg*
> *salt & freshly ground black pepper*
> *3 tablespoons chopped fresh parsley*
> *oil, for shallow frying*
> *1 quantity Yogurt Tartar (see page 259), to serve*

5

1 Put the nuts and the walnut oil into a food processor and process, starting and stopping the machine until coarsely ground. Transfer to a large mixing bowl, add the remaining ingredients and mix well. If the mixture seems too soft, add more breadcrumbs.

5

2 Heat the frying oil in a large heavy-based pan and fry spoonfuls of the mixture for 4–5 minutes on each side or until golden-brown.

8-10

3 Drain well on kitchen paper. Arrange the drained rissoles on a heated serving dish, pour the Yogurt Tartar over and serve with a rice or burgul pilaff.

3

AUBERGINE IN MISO

Miso is one of the most important *fonds de cuisine* of the Japanese kitchen. It is a paste made out of fermented soya beans and malted grains – either rice, wheat or barley. Miso comes in different colours, from pale yellow to reddish and dark brown. It can be found in all Japanese shops and some oriental and health food shops also carry it. There is no substitute to miso, so buy it on your next food shopping expedition. Tightly covered, it can be kept in the fridge for up to 3 months.

For this dish any variety of aubergine can be used but try to shop around for small white, light purple or green baby aubergines.

Serve hot on a bed of rice, kway teow (wide rice noodles) or plump, yellow fresh Chinese egg noddles. Serves 4.

30 minutes

juice of 1 lemon
750 g / 1½ lb aubergines
1 large red pepper
1 large green pepper
3 tablespoons sesame or peanut oil
6 large cloves of garlic, peeled & halved
2.5 cm / 1 in piece of fresh ginger, finely chopped
1–2 red or green chillies, sliced into thin rings
2 tablespoons miso
1 tablespoon dark soy sauce
50 ml / 2 fl.oz stock or water
2 tablespoons sake or very dry sherry

5

3 tablespoons sesame seeds

1 Put the lemon juice into a large bowl. Cut the unpeeled aubergines into wedges measuring 5 x 2.5 cm/2 x 1 in and make 2–3 shallow cuts in the skin of each wedge. If baby aubergines are used, either halve or quarter according to size. Add the sliced aubergine to the lemon juice and mix well so all the slices are coated with juice.

5-7

3-5

2 Cut the peppers in half, discard the seeds, remove the membrane and slice into 5 x 2.5 cm/2 x 1 in chunks.

3 Heat the oil in a wok or a heavy-based frying pan and add the garlic. Fry over a high heat until the garlic starts to brown. Add the ginger and the chilli and fry for a few seconds. Add the aubergine and peppers and cook, stirring constantly to prevent sticking, for 3–4 minutes.

5

4 Add the miso, soy sauce and stock or water, reduce the heat and simmer, stirring frequently, for about 8–10 minutes. Increase the heat to maximum, add the sake or sherry and boil rapidly for a few seconds. Switch off the heat, transfer to a heated serving dish and sprinkle with the sesame seeds which have been previously roasted in a dry frying pan until they emit a pleasant nutty aroma. Serve hot with rice or noodles accompanied by Fennel & Pink Grapefruit Salad (see page 94) and red wine.

12-15

SWEET & SOUR STUFFED TOFU

This dish calls for golden slices of deep-fried tofu, which are available in most oriental food stores. If you can't find them they are very easily and quickly prepared at home.

To make them, buy fresh tofu and cut into 4 cm/1 ½ in thick slices. Drain and dry well with kitchen paper. Heat the oil in a deep-fryer and fry the slices, a few at a time, for about 5 minutes or until evenly golden all over. Drain well on kitchen paper. Allow to cool and use as directed. Serves 4.

30 minutes

2 carrots, peeled
3 sticks of celery, leaves included
2.5 cm/1 in piece of peeled ginger
2 cloves of garlic, peeled
100 g/4 oz fried tofu slices per serving
1 quantity Lemon Grass & Chilli Sauce (see page
*   262) with 1 tablespoon sugar or honey added*

5

1

1   Heat the oven to 200°C/400°F/Gas Mark 6.

2   Put the carrots, celery, ginger and garlic into a food processor and process at high speed, starting and stopping the machine until the vegetables are finely chopped but not puréed.

3

3   Make a deep slash in the narrow side of each tofu slice to create a pocket, and stuff it with the vegetable mixture. Arrange the slices in a deep baking dish, pour over the Lemon Grass and Chilli Sauce and bake for 15–20 minutes. Serve sprinkled with chopped coriander and a little of the cooking liquid on a bed of rice or noodles.

20-25

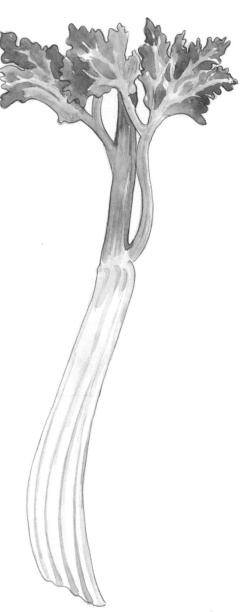

MIDDLE-EASTERN RICE

Very good rice is hard to come by and the polished, pre-cooked variety, although it cooks very easily, is usually tasteless. Rice is essential for biryanis, pilaffs, risottos and paellas but as an accompaniment to main courses it can often be rather insipid and boring, unless of exceptional quality. The following recipe is very flavoursome and comes from the Middle East. It presents a novel and interesting way of serving rice. Serves 4.

30 minutes

4 tablespoons peanut or sesame oil
100 g/4 oz spaghetti
500 g/1 lb fragrant long-grain rice
1 litre/2 pints water
1½–2 teaspoons salt
50 g/2 oz pine-nuts

2

1   Heat the oil in a heavy-based saucepan. Break the spaghetti into even 2.5 cm/1 in strands and add to the oil. Fry over a high heat, stirring all the time, until the pasta is evenly browned. Add the rice and continue frying until the rice turns opaquely white. Add the water and the salt, reduce the heat to minimum and cook, covered, for about 15–20 minutes until all the liquid is absorbed and the rice is cooked and fluffy.

25

2   Transfer to a heated serving dish and sprinkle with pine-nuts previously browned in a little oil. Serve immediately.

3

POLENTA

In North America pre-cooked polenta is readily available in most supermarket chains. It comes as a sausage-shaped parcel and all you have to do is slice it, fry or grill it and serve with your favourite topping. This product has recently reached the British market but, alas, is still rare. By now, however, most shops carry an instant polenta which is just as good. To make it, follow the manufacturer's directions.

The classic way of making this south Italian speciality is relatively easy and quick, although constant stirring is essential because it tends to burn easily and stick to the bottom of the pan. Serves 4.

35 minutes

1 litre/2 pints water
2 teaspoons salt
225 g/8 oz polenta or yellow cornmeal
50 ml/2 fl.oz melted butter or good olive oil

2

1   Bring the water to the boil in a large, heavy-based saucepan and add the salt. Sprinkle in the polenta, stirring all the time to prevent lumps. Reduce the heat to minimum and simmer, stirring frequently, for about 25 minutes, until the mixture is thick enough to stand a spoon in.

28

2   Either serve immediately with Fresh Tomato Sauce (see page 267), or turn the polenta on to a buttered or oiled baking sheet or marble slab. Dip your hands in cold water and spread the polenta into an even 2.5–4 cm/1–1½ in layer. Allow to cool.

(30)

3   When completely cold, stamp or cut the polenta into the required shapes. Brush the polenta shapes with melted butter or oil and grill, bake or fry. Serve hot with a sauce, with freshly grated Parmesan cheese or use to make the Polenta 'Pizzas' (see page 73), for which you will need 12 x 7.5 cm/3 in discs.

5

DESSERTS

SHARON FRUIT SOUFFLÉS

Sharon fruit is also known as persimmon or kaki fruit. They start reaching the market at the beginning of autumn. Although they do not have a very pronounced flavour, they are exceedingly sweet and very pleasant to eat. They add a bright orange colour to fruit or savoury salads, and when very ripe and peeled are easily made into a smooth purée.

The new variety can be eaten when still hard but is most delicious when very soft, chilled, cut in half and eaten with a spoon.

Sliced hard sharon fruit, dressed in olive oil or nut vinaigrette, makes an interesting salad. Serves 4.

30 minutes

6 soft, ripe sharon fruit
2 tablespoons Amaretto liqueur
100 g/4 oz mascarpone cheese
75 g/3 oz ground almonds
1 egg, separated
1 tablespoon clear honey
5 *pinch of salt*

1 1 Heat the oven to 200°C/400°F/Gas Mark 6.

2 Slice the tops off the sharon fruit and scoop out the flesh, creating little baskets. Keep the tops for lids and
5 sprinkle each basket with a few drops of the Amaretto.

3 Put the scooped-out flesh into a food processor and add the cheese, ground almonds, egg yolk, honey and
3 remaining Amaretto. Process at high speed for a few seconds. Transfer to a mixing bowl.

4 In another bowl, add a pinch of salt to the egg white and whisk to a firm, soft snow. Fold the egg white gently into the fruit purée and pile the fluffy mixture into the baskets. Cover with the lids and bake in the pre-heated
15-20 oven for 12–15 minutes. Serve immediately.

SUMMER FRUIT PARCELS

Summer does not really start until berries appear in the market, turning fruit-sellers' displays into a riot of colour. Berries also add colour and flavour to both sweet and savoury dishes. Try to include sour-sweet, firmer berries in stews, remembering to add them in the last stages of cooking. They go very well with sweet potatoes, mushrooms and even the cabbage family. Or decorate cold salads with bunches of red and white currants, blueberries, raspberries or whatever berry is available.

Summer fruit is synonymous with Summer Pudding which is the most delicious way of utilizing the glut. The following uses the same combination of fruit, creating a crustless, hot, luscious and flamboyant version of this classic. Serves 4.

25-40 minutes

75 g/3 oz butter, melted
500 g/1 lb 2 oz assorted summer fruit
3 tablespoons moist brown sugar
6 tablespoons good brandy or cognac
1 vanilla pod or cinnamon stick, cut into 6 pieces
6 cloves
6 small strips of lemon zest
1 quantity Raspberry Sauce (see page 273) or Custard Sauce (see page 273), to serve

5-20

1

1   Heat the oven to 200°C/400°F/Gas Mark 6.

2   Generously butter 6 x 20 cm/8 in circles of kitchen foil or parchment. Gently mix the fruit with the sugar and brandy. Divide the fruit equally among the circles, placing it at the centre. Arrange the vanilla or cinnamon, cloves and lemon peel on top and close the parcels by drawing the edges up and crimping them together firmly, creating a neat pouch.

5

3   Place on a baking tray and bake in the pre-heated oven for 8–10 minutes. Serve the hot parcel on a pool of cool fruit sauce or custard. Supply sharp pointed knives which will allow each diner to open the parcel and enjoy the full blast of the heady, fruity aroma.

10-12

CRUSTLESS PEACH & ALMOND PIE

Many other fruits can be used for this dessert, such as pears, apples, figs, apricots or plums. It is very good served hot but even better just slightly warm. Serve with ice cream, custard or cream. Serves 4.

35 minutes

8 large peaches or nectarines
butter for greasing
2–3 tablespoons ground almonds or breadcrumbs, for coating
3 tablespoons apricot jam, sieved
crème fraîche or cream, to serve (optional)
For the filling
150 g/6 oz softened butter
75 g/3 oz caster sugar
1 teaspoon grated orange rind
1 teaspoon grated lemon rind
3 eggs (size 3)
150 g/6 oz ground almonds
3 tablespoons plain flour
a few drops of natural bitter almond essence
2 teaspoons orange-blossom water
2 tablespoons orange liqueur

5

1

1 Heat your oven to 200°C/400°F/Gas Mark 6.

2 First make the filling. Put the butter and sugar into the bowl of your mixer and whisk at high speed for 1 minute or until the butter is light and fluffy. Gradually add the remaining filling ingredients, and mix to a smooth cream.

5

3 If peaches are used, plunge them into boiling water, lift out, refresh with iced water and peel. Nectarines do not need peeling. Halve the fruit, remove the stones and cut into thin slices.

5

4 Butter a 22.5 cm/9 in deep flan dish well, sprinkle with the ground almonds or breadcrumbs and knock out the excess. Pour the creamed mixture into the dish and spread out evenly with a small spatula or the back of a spoon. Arrange the sliced fruit on top in a decorative pattern.

5

5 Bake in the pre-heated oven for 15–20 minutes or until set. Meanwhile, in a small saucepan, melt the apricot jam together with 2 tablespoons water. Bring to the boil. Use to brush over the flan as soon as it comes out of the oven. Either serve hot or allow to cool down and serve just warm with a dollop of crème fraîche, double cream or, best of all, fresh clotted cream.

15-20

SCENTED PEARS

The inspiration for the following recipe is a classic Provençal dish which was quoted by Roger Vergé – a true Mediterranean whose food reflects the tradition and flavour of the region. In the original pears or peaches are flavoured with black pepper and bay leaves. Fresh lavender sprigs – another Mediterranean favourite – also work very well. If you do not have lavender growing in your garden, use 1-2 tablespoons dried lavender flowers instead.

This dish can be served hot but it is much better to let the pears cool in their cooking liquor and serve them at room temperature. For extra richness, thick cream could be served. Serves 4.

30 minutes

1 bottle full-bodied soft red wine
6 tablespoons lavender (or any other fragrant) honey
2 tablespoons black peppercorns, tied in a muslin bag
6 sprigs of lavender flowers
juice and zest of 1 lemon
6 ripe pears, peeled with the stem attached
6 sprigs of lavender flower (optional) and mint to decorate

5

5

1 Combine the wine, honey, peppercorns, lavender flowers and lemon juice and zest in a large, heavy bottomed pan. Bring to the boil and cook for 2 minutes.

20

2 Reduce the heat, add the pears and simmer, very gently, for 10 minutes. Remove from the heat and allow to cool. Serve the pears with a little of the cooking liquid and decorated with the lavender blossom and mint.

WARM POACHED PEARS IN WINE WITH MASCARPONE

30+ minutes

Poaching pears in wine is a delightful – and traditional – idea. Keep them in jars in your kitchen store cupboard, and each pear will make a delicious treat! Serves 4.

4 firm conference pears
1 cinnamon stick
1 vanilla pod, split in half lengthways
3 tablespoons caster sugar
zest of ½ orange
zest of ½ lemon
900 ml/1½ pints red wine
2   *150 g/5 oz mascarpone cheese*

1   Peel, halve and remove the pips from the pears and place in a pan where they will fit tightly. Add the cinnamon, the vanilla pod, the sugar and the citrus zest and cover with the wine. Weight the pears down with a plate, so that they will not float as the juices simmer, bring gently to the boil, then simmer for 10–15 minutes.

20-25

2   Remove the plate, carefully take out the pears and keep them warm. Turn the heat up and boil the juices until they have reduced by half.

8-10

3   Arrange the pears on serving plates, drizzle on some of the reduced poaching liquid, and accompany with a spoonful of mascarpone. Delicious with cantuccini biscuits (Tuscan almond biscuits).

1

BAKED PEACHES WITH MACAROON FILLING

Ripe juicy peaches are delicious on their own, but this way they are even better. Try to find white peaches at the end of spring which are delicate in flavour and beautifully perfumed. Serves 4.

30 minutes

4 peaches, halved & stones removed
1 teaspoon amaretto liqueur
6 macaroons or amaretti biscuits, crushed
1 tablespoon ground almonds
50 g/2 oz unsalted butter

3

3

1   With a spoon scoop out a little flesh from the centre of each peach half and gently mash it.

2   In a bowl mix the peach flesh with the liqueur, the macaroons or amaretti and the ground almonds, then spoon back into the peaches.

4-5

3   Grease an ovenproof dish with a little of the butter. Arrange the stuffed peach halves in it and dot with the remaining butter.

3

4   Bake in a pre-heated oven at 220°C/425°F/Gas Mark 7 for about 15 minutes until the peaches are golden-brown and heated through.

15

1

5   Serve hot with a little cold zabaglione (page 226) or some double cream.

FLAMING PAWPAW

This is a dish designed to impress. It is spectacular in appearance, delicious and extremely easy to prepare. Be careful to select fully ripe pawpaw and keep some of the black pips for decoration; they have an amazingly refreshing, pleasant flavour. Serve accompanied with well-chilled fruity, semi-sweet white wine, such as a Riesling.

Like mango, pawpaw can easily be made into a smooth purée and green under-ripe fruit can be used to make a delicious savoury salad. Pawpaw is good for you as it contains a large amount of papain, an enzyme which plays an important part in digestion. Serves 4.

25 minutes

6 ratafia biscuits
4 tablespoons rum
3 ripe, medium pawpaws, chilled
juice & grated rind of 1 lemon
225 g/8 oz curd cheese, chilled
100 g/4 oz crème fraîche or strained Greek yogurt, chilled
2 tablespoons moist molasses sugar or honey
a few drops of rose- or orange-blossom water
2 tablespoons mixed peel or chopped, candied orange peel

_5_

_5_
1 Soak the ratafias in the rum.

_5_
2 Halve the pawpaws, remove the pips and save for decoration. Scoop out some of the flesh to increase the cavity, chop it coarsely and reserve. Sprinkle the hollows with a few drops of lemon juice and refrigerate.

3 Put the curd cheese together with the crème fraîche or yogurt, sugar or honey, lemon juice and rind, rose- or orange-blossom water into a food processor. Process for 1 minute then transfer to a mixing bowl. Fold in the chopped pawpaw and mixed peel. Pile into the pawpaw hollows and decorate with a few pips. Place a soaked ratafia on each, set alight and serve

_10_
flaming.

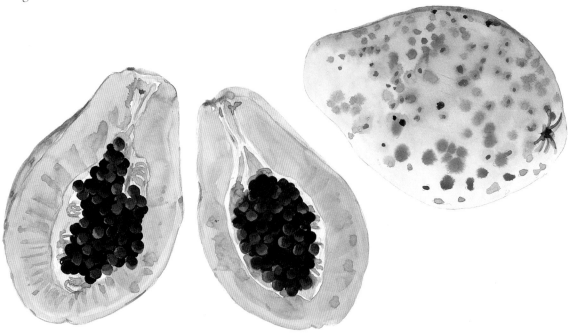

ZABAGLIONE

15 minutes

Zabaglione is a great invention! A terrific pick-me-up if you do not have a problem with cholesterol. When you have mastered the technique, experiment with different wines. Serves 4.

2

4 egg yolks
4 tablespoons caster sugar
4 tablespoons Marsala wine
3–4 tablespoons sweet white wine

3-5

1 Set a mixing bowl over a pan of boiling water. In the bowl, vigorously whisk the egg yolks with the sugar over a medium heat until the mixture begins to thicken and lighten. It is important that the heat under the bowl is not too high or the mixture will curdle.

8-10

2 Whisk in the Marsala and white wine in small quantities at regular intervals until both have been incorporated (the mixture should be thick and velvety, not frothy). Then pour into glasses and serve with sponge fingers or fresh strawberries, ripe apricots and figs to dip in.

NOTE: Zabaglione can also be served cold. After preparing it as instructed above, place the hot mixing bowl over ice and keep stirring or lightly whisking until the zabaglione is completely cold. Use as it is or as a sauce.

APRICOT & MARSALA FOOL

15 minutes

It is very important that the apricots are ripe. If you cannot find ripe ones, try cooking them instead (see note below). Serves 4.

5

6 very ripe apricots, stoned
1 tablespoon icing sugar
2 tablespoons Marsala wine
300 ml / 10 fl.oz double cream
1 tablespoon toasted flaked almonds

1

1 Blend the apricots, icing sugar and Marsala in a liquidizer.

3-4

2 Whip the cream in a bowl until it holds its shape, then fold in the apricot mixture.

5

3 Spoon into serving glasses or ramekins, sprinkle with the almonds and serve.

NOTE: To cook unripe apricots, stone and quarter them, add 2–3 tablespoons of water, a couple of tablespoons of icing sugar and a squeeze of lemon and cook over a low heat until the apricots are soft and translucent. Then liquidize, leave to cool and proceed from Step 2 of the recipe.

TOFFEE BAKED APPLES

Marsala wine probably does not feature in many toffee recipes, but somehow it is not out of place here. John Woodhouse first produced it in Sicily in the late eighteenth century and it is said to have invigorated Nelson and his royal navy! Serves 4.

30 minutes

4 tablespoons soft brown sugar
100 g/4 oz unsalted butter
2 tablespoons golden syrup
1 tablespoon treacle
2 tablespoons rum or Marsala wine
450 ml/15 fl.oz double cream
4 Bramley apples, halved horizontally
25 g/1 oz toasted flaked almonds

5

8-10

1 Melt the sugar with the butter, golden syrup and treacle in a flameproof dish over a low heat. When the mixture is well blended and starts to bubble, add the rum or Marsala and 300 ml/10 fl.oz of the cream. Mix well and bring to the boil.

2 Remove the dish from the heat and place the apples in it, cut side down. Bake in a pre-heated oven at 220°C/425°F/Gas Mark 7 for 8–10 minutes.

10-12

3 Remove the apples from the oven and reassemble them. Pour over the cooking juices and the remaining cream. Sprinkle with the almonds and enjoy!

3

WARM BERRIES ON TOASTED PANETTONE WITH CLOTTED CREAM

Throughout the Christmas season hundreds of panettoni dangle from the ceilings and shelves of most Italian delicatessens. This traditional cake is in effect a light bread dough enriched with butter, candied peel and sultanas. At breakfast or teatime try toasting left-over slices spread with honey. Serves 4.

20 minutes

75 g/3 oz redcurrant jelly
juice of 1 lemon
1–2 tablespoons brandy
4 slices of panettone
75 g/3 oz strawberries, hulled & halved
75 g/3 oz blueberries, washed & drained
75 g/3 oz blackberries, washed & drained
75 g/3 oz raspberries, washed & drained
icing sugar for dusting

10

4 tablespoons clotted cream

2-3

1 Gently melt the redcurrant jelly with the lemon juice and brandy in a frying pan.

3-4

2 Meanwhile, toast the panettone slices on both sides and keep warm.

3 When the jelly has melted and is well blended with the other ingredients, add all the berries and toss gently, coating the fruit with the hot syrupy mixture.

3

4 Place the toasted panettone on serving plates, spoon on the hot fruit and dust with icing sugar. Serve with a dollop of clotted cream.

2-3

BLUEBERRY PANCAKES WITH CRÈME FRAÎCHE

Use fresh fruit, not frozen or tinned, not just for better flavour but also because the pancakes will become too wet otherwise. Serves 4.

30 minutes

100 g/4 oz plain flour
1 tablespoon caster sugar
2 tablespoons double cream
2 eggs, separated
grated rind of 1 lemon
225 ml/8 fl.oz milk
unsalted butter
1 punnet of fresh blueberries, washed & drained
4–6 tablespoons maple syrup

5

4 tablespoons crème fraîche

1

1 Sift the flour into a bowl, mix in the sugar and make a well in the centre.

2 In a separate bowl mix the double cream, egg yolks, lemon rind and milk. Pour into the well in the flour and mix thoroughly, using a small whisk or a wooden spoon, to make a smooth batter.

2-3

3 Whisk the egg whites until stiff. Gently spoon a third of them into the flour to loosen the texture, then fold in the rest.

2-3

4 Melt a small knob of butter in a 15 cm/6 in frying pan. Pour in one-quarter of the batter (the pancake should not be more than 1 cm/½ in thick) and sprinkle with some blueberries. When small bubbles begin to break on the surface, flip the pancake over and cook for another minute or two. Slide on to a warm serving plate, drizzle with maple syrup and keep warm.

5

5 Make 3 more pancakes with the remaining batter in the same way, then serve with a dollop of crème fraîche: DELICIOUS!

12-15

HAZELNUT PANCAKES SERVED WITH QUICK APRICOT JAM

These wonderfully light but filling pancakes are an ideal sweet for a winter meal.

The ground hazelnuts can be used raw. But for a fuller flavour, lightly roast the ground nuts in a dry frying pan until they begin to emit a pleasant roasted aroma.

If a coarser, more textured pancake is preferred, use whole, lightly roasted nuts. Put them into a food processor and process, switching the machine off and on until the required texture is achieved. I sometimes vary the flavouring by using vanilla essence or orange-blossom water instead of cinnamon.

The pancakes are best served hot, accompanied with lashings of clotted or any other thick cream or Greek yogurt. Serves 4.

30 minutes

5 eggs (size 3)
225 g/8 oz ground hazelnuts
3 tablespoons plain flour
1 teaspoon baking powder
2 tablespoons clear honey
100 ml/4 fl.oz milk
½ teaspoon natural bitter almond essence
2 teaspoons ground cinnamon
butter for frying
icing sugar for dusting
½ quantity Quick Apricot 'Jam' Sauce (see page 272) & thick cream, to serve

5

1 Mix all the ingredients to a smooth, thickish batter in a mixing bowl. In a frying pan heat a little butter and fry spoonfuls of the batter for 2–3 minutes on each side or until the pancakes are pale golden-brown and risen. Keep hot while frying the remaining pancakes.

20

2 Arrange on a heated serving plate and spread each pancake with apricot jam, dust with sugar and top with a dollop of cream. Serve immediately.

3

CHOCOLATE & HAZELNUT TRUFFLE CUPS

Hazelnuts are ever-popular, and they mix with chocolate very well. If you ever find yourself in Turin, try Gianduiotti, oddly shaped hazelnut chocolates that are the best combination of the two ingredients. Serves 4.

30 minutes

170 g/6 oz dark chocolate
2–3 tablespoons rum or brandy
100 g/4 oz hazelnuts, roasted, skins removed & roughly chopped
2 egg whites
2 tablespoons caster sugar
5 *300 ml/10 fl.oz double cream*

1 Melt the chocolate with the rum or brandy and the hazelnuts in a bowl over a pan of simmering water. When
15 melted, remove from the heat and cool, stirring occasionally until lukewarm.

3 2 Whisk the egg whites until they hold their shape, then add the sugar and whisk until stiff. Set aside.

3 3 Whisk the double cream until thick.

4 Fold the egg whites into the chocolate mixture and mix well, then fold in the cream. Spoon into serving cups,
3-4 chill for 10 minutes and serve.

MELON DELIGHT

Although melons are available almost all year round, watermelons appear only in summer. The fruit, which can reach an enormous size, makes the most refreshing and easiest sweet possible when chilled. Serve it cut into thick slices or elegantly as cubes in a basket made from its skin, accompanied by fresh salted cheese which brings out its flavour beautifully.

To choose ripe watermelon, rap the fruit with your knuckle. If it sounds hollow, the fruit should be ripe and sweet. For this recipe, select one of the new seedless varieties of watermelon, which will save you the bother of de-seeding the fruit. Serves 4.

25 minutes

1 kg/2¼ lb watermelon, de-seeded if necessary, well chilled
2 tablespoons clear honey
juice of 1 lemon
3 tablespoons orange liqueur, such as Grand Marnier or Cointreau
1 tablespoon chopped fresh mint
1 medium honeydew, Galia or cantaloupe melon, well chilled
1 medium charentais melon

5

sprigs of fresh mint, to decorate

10

1 Place the watermelon in a food processor, add the honey, lemon juice, liqueur and chopped mint and process at high speed for 1 minute. Use a melon baller to scoop neat balls out of the two other melons.

10

2 To assemble, mask each serving plate with the watermelon sauce, arrange the melon balls on top and decorate with sprigs of mint.

CHOCOLATE FONDUE

The best chocolate to use for the sauce is the unsweetened variety, which can be difficult to get. Use chocolate with high cocoa solids content (above 50 per cent) or the best bittersweet chocolate you can get. Melting good-quality chocolate can be very tricky, if any moisture gets in it turns, irretrievably, to an unappetizing oily mass. Chocolate burns easily so never boil the sauce.

Any fruit can be used: select it according to colour, texture and availability. Strawberries, cape gooseberries, cherries, melon and pawpaw are particularly good. Serves 4.

30 minutes

350 g/12 oz good bitter chocolate, broken into pieces
about 75 g/3 oz–100 g/4 oz seasonal fruit per serving, peeled & sliced if necessary
150 ml/5 fl.oz double cream
75 g/3 oz dark molasses sugar
1 heaped tablespoon good cocoa powder
2 teaspoons orange-blossom water or a few drops of almond essence

5

3 tablespoons rum, brandy, cognac or your favourite liqueur

10

1 Place the chocolate in a double boiler and leave to melt over a gentle heat.

5

2 Arrange the fruit on a large dish lined with crushed ice and keep cold.

3 Bring the cream to the boil in a large saucepan, add the sugar and simmer, stirring frequently to prevent scorching, for about 5 minutes, over a medium heat. Add to the melted chocolate and mix well. Add the

10

remaining ingredients, stir well and serve, in a fondue dish, with the fresh fruit and long forks or skewers.

BANANA, APPLE & CHOCOLATE CRUMBLE

Crumble: what a great invention! Try different combinations throughout the seasons – peach and apricot, raspberry and apple, pear and dried figs, apple, orange and sultanas. A meal in themselves! Serves 4.

30 minutes

2 large bananas, peeled & sliced
2 medium Bramley apples, peeled, cored & cut into chunks
1 tablespoon rum
juice of ½ lemon
1 tablespoon icing sugar plus extra for dusting
2 tablespoons grated dark chocolate

For the crumble
175 g/6 oz plain flour
150 g/5 oz cold unsalted butter, cut into cubes
50 g/2 oz ground hazelnuts
50 g/2 oz soft brown sugar

10

1 In a bowl mix the bananas and apples with the rum, lemon juice and icing sugar, then pack tightly into an ovenproof dish, sprinkle with the grated chocolate and set aside.

3

2 Make the crumble: place the flour in a food processor and activate the blade, then add the butter a piece at a time. Toss the mixture in a bowl and fold in the hazelnuts and sugar.

2

2

3 Spoon the crumble on to the fruit, covering the entire surface neatly and pressing the mixture on to the fruit.

4 Bake in a pre-heated oven at 220°C/425°F/Gas Mark 7 for 15–20 minutes (the juices should bubble around the edges and the topping should be golden-brown).

15-20

1

5 Serve with pouring cream or ice-cream.

DATE, SULTANA & ALMOND FILO PARCELS WITH VANILLA ICE-CREAM

Crispy pastry, luxurious filling – even if you have never used filo pastry you must try this recipe! Serves 4.

30 minutes

1 tablespoon water
1 tablespoon brandy
grated rind of ½ orange
2 tablespoons sultanas
12 fresh, ripe dates, stoned & thinly sliced
75 g/3 oz almonds, roasted & fairly finely chopped
6 sheets of filo pastry
100 g/4 oz unsalted butter, melted
icing sugar for dusting
4 scoops vanilla ice-cream

5

6-7

1 Heat the water with the brandy and orange rind in a saucepan. Add the sultanas and simmer for 4–5 minutes, then drain off excess juices and leave to cool.

1

2 In a bowl mix together the dates, almonds and cooled sultanas. Set aside.

3 With a pastry brush, brush one half of one sheet of filo pastry with the melted butter. Fold the unbuttered half over the buttered one, then brush again with butter. Cut the folded, twice-buttered sheet of pastry in half lengthways.

3

1

4 Place a spoonful of the date mixture at the base of each strip of pastry. Gently fold in the edges of each strip, butter lightly, then roll the pastry to make a neat barrel-shaped parcel.

5 Proceed from Step 3 until all the pastry and the filling are used up. Then place the parcels on a baking tray and bake in a pre-heated oven at 220°C/425°F/Gas Mark 7 for about 8–10 minutes or until golden-brown.

18-23

7 When the parcels are ready, remove from the oven and place on serving dishes. Dust with icing sugar and serve with the vanilla ice-cream. SCRUMMY!

1

STUFFED DATES

25 minutes

This recipe was probably written down 1800 years ago, and is attributed to the legendary Roman food writer, Epicus. In the original, the stuffed figs were coated with salt and fried in honey to produce a rather strange flavour. Served here accompanied with cream as a tempting dessert or on their own as an interesting Christmas *petit-fours*, these dates are always appreciated! Serves 4.

150 g/6 oz peeled pistachio nuts (reserve 1 nut for each date)
1-2 tablespoons fragrant honey
50 g/2 oz – 75 g/3 oz ground almonds
3-4 fresh dates per person, stones removed
2 teaspoons orange blossom or rose water

10

2-3

1 Place the pistachios and honey in a food processor and process at high speed until coarsely ground.

2 Transfer the content to a mixing bowl. Add the ground almonds and mix well. If the mixture is too loose add some more ground almonds.

2-3

3 Stuff a little of the mixture into each date, and decorate with a pistachio nut. Either arrange on individual serving plates on a pool of thick cream or serve in paper cases as *petit-fours*.

10

STUFFED FIGS

Figs are forever associated with sensual, cool, end-of-summer evenings. One of the first fruits cultivated by man, the magnificent fig tree still dominates the landscape of large parts of the Mediterranean, from Spain right round to Morroco.

Figs are best eaten simply. Peeled or unpeeled, they can be accompanied by a strongly flavoured cheese; or serve them as a first course stuffed with feta or any other salty goat or sheep's milk cheese flavoured with fresh chopped mint.

Select figs that are unblemished, very ripe and just firm to the touch. This dish is decorated with fresh bay leaves which, as well as providing a luscious green decoration, add their pungent smell. Serves 4.

20 minutes

> *250 g/8 oz mascarpone, well chilled*
> *75 g/3 oz glacé mixed peel, finely chopped*
> *1-2 tablespoons good honey*
> *1 tablespoon grappa, marc or brandy*
> *a few drops of orange blossom water*
> *2-3 figs for each portion*
> *bay leaves for decoration*

5

2

1 Place all the ingredients with the exception of the figs into a mixing bowl and mix well.

10

2 Slice the figs across and across again, creating 4-petalled 'flowers' which are still joined at the stem end. Fill each of these with the cheese mixture. Decorate and chill for at least 2 hours before serving.

GLAZED FIGS

In early autumn figs start to come into the market. These ancient, succulent and erotic fruit are mostly available in two varieties: a pale green, 'white-skinned' variety which has pale, glistening, honey-gold flesh and a large dark purple variety which has luscious pink flesh.

Figs are best eaten simply raw, peeled or unpeeled, accompanied by a strongly flavoured cheese. Or serve them as a first course, stuffed with feta or other salty goat's or sheep's cheese which has been previously flavoured with chopped fresh mint.

When selecting figs make sure that they are unblemished, very ripe and just firm to the touch. It is difficult to ripen figs at home. The best one can do is wrap them individually in a piece of newspaper and hope for the best! Serves 4.

25 minutes

18 just-ripe purple figs
225 ml/8 fl.oz medium or dry sherry or madeira
5 cardamom pods, broken
½ cinnamon stick
2 tablespoons butter
6 sprigs of mint
clotted cream or fromage frais, to serve

5

5

1 Make 3 cuts in each fig so that the sections are still joined at the stem end.

2 Bring the sherry or madeira to the boil in a large frying pan, add the cardamom and cinnamon and boil hard for a minute or two. Add the figs and simmer for 2–3 minutes, turning once. Lift the figs out and keep warm.

5

3 Return the pan to the heat and boil hard until the liquid is reduced by half (about 5 minutes). Add the butter and continue boiling, beating all the time, until a thick and shiny sauce is achieved (about 1–2 minutes). Pour over the figs, decorate with sprigs of mint and serve with cream or fromage frais.

7-8

GINGERED MANGO PURÉE

A good mango is one of nature's presents. It should be ripe, just soft, juicy, not too stringy and with a heavenly, resinous, sweet aroma. Mangoes vary greatly in shape, size and colour. Some remain green or green flashed with red when ripe, others turn red, orange and gold.

Ripe sweet mangoes can very easily be turned into a flavoursome purée. Sliced fresh mango makes a wonderful breakfast. Unripe green mangoes are delicious served as a savoury salad and make a superb chutney.

The mango has a large, flattish stone to which the flesh adheres stubbornly. To prepare, slice through the mango as close to the stone as possible. First cut the flesh from around the stone and then make even criss-cross cuts through each section, being careful not to damage the skin. Bend each section to separate the cubes and remove each with a sharp knife or a spoon. Serves 4.

20 minutes

3 large, ripe mangoes, well chilled
juice of 1 lemon
2.5 cm / 1 in piece of fresh ginger, peeled & finely chopped or grated
75 g / 3 oz crystallized ginger, chopped
grated rind of 1 lemon
150 g / 5 oz crème fraîche or yogurt, well chilled
3 tablespoons good clear honey, chilled
50 g / 2 oz slivered & roasted almonds or pine-nuts

10

3-5

1 Peel the mangoes, remove the stones and put the flesh into a food processor. Add the lemon juice and process at high speed for 1 minute. If the mango is stringy, pass the purée through a sieve.

2 Transfer to a mixing bowl, add the gingers and lemon rind and mix well. Divide the purée among 6 serving bowls. Top each with a dollop of crème fraîche or yogurt, drizzle with the chilled honey, sprinkle with nuts and serve.

5-7

AMARETTI & RASPBERRY CUSTARD

Amaretti are traditional biscuits from Piedmont and Lombardy, made with a mixture of sweet and bitter almonds. Serves 4.

25 minutes

600 ml/1 pint double cream
1 teaspoon vanilla essence or 1 vanilla pod, split in half lengthways
6 egg yolks
100 g/4 oz caster sugar
1 tablespoon marsala wine
170 g/6 oz fresh raspberries
3   *6 amaretti biscuits, crushed*

3-4   1 In a small heavy saucepan gently heat the cream with the vanilla essence or pod.

3   2 Meanwhile, whisk the yolks with the sugar until well blended.

         3 When the cream is about to reach boiling point, remove from the heat. Remove the vanilla pod, if used, and scrape out the little black seeds. Return the seeds to the cream. Pour the cream over the egg yolk mixture and
1-2   stir well.

         4 Return the egg and cream to the pan and place in another pan filled with boiling water (or use a double
10-12   saucepan). Cook the custard until thick, stirring continuously.

         5 When the custard is ready, place a few raspberries at the bottom of 4 ramekins or other serving dishes, sprinkle with some of the crushed amaretti, then pour over the warm custard. Sprinkle with the remaining amaretti,
5-10   leave to stand for 5–10 minutes and serve.

NOTE: If prepared the day before, leave to chill in the refrigerator and the custard will set. You can then top the dessert with a thin layer of caramel.

Amaretti & Raspberry
Custard and Strawberry &
Peach Fruit Salad in
Red Wine (see page 255)

CARAMELIZED GRAPEFRUIT

The combination of bitter-sweet grapefruit with caramelized sugar is refreshing and different. Try, in season, to use pomelos, which like grapefruit come in white- and pink-fleshed varieties. The pomelo is one of the ancient varieties of citrus from which the grapefruit was developed. It is larger than grapefruit and its flesh is less juicy and composed of a large number of well-defined 'bottles' which pop and crunch in your mouth. The new varieties are sweet and do not have the bitterness of grapefruit. Serves 4.

30 minutes

3 large pink grapefruits or pomelos
3 large white grapefruits
3 tablespoons orange or grapefruit marmalade
1–2 teaspoons orange-blossom water
3 tablespoons moist brown sugar

3

1

1 Heat the grill to maximum.

2 To segment the grapefruit, cut a slice both top and bottom to expose the flesh. Lay the grapefruit, cut side up, on a chopping board and then, using a serrated knife, slice away the peel, exposing the flesh and removing all traces of the white pith. Hold the peeled grapefruit in the palm of your hand and, using a sharp knife, slice along the vertical membrane lines, leaving a perfectly peeled segment. The same technique is used to segment oranges and pomelos. When all the segments are removed, squeeze the juice out of the flesh and reserve. Arrange the segments on a well-buttered ovenproof serving dish.

15

3 In a small saucepan combine the marmalade and the reserved juice and orange-blossom water. Bring to the boil and boil rapidly for 4–5 minutes until reduced to a glossy sauce, thick enough to coat a spoon. Pour it over the grapefruit. Sprinkle with sugar and caramelize under the hot grill.

8-10

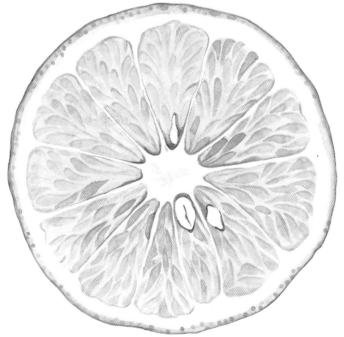

ORANGE & ALMOND CUSTARD

This light and tasty custard comes from Spain and contains two of the most favourite Mediterranean ingredients – oranges and almonds.

The addition of orange blossom water (although not essential) gives this dish its characteristic perfume. It can be easily bought in any good Mediterranean or Middle Eastern store. Serves 4.

30 minutes

30 ml/12 fl.oz freshly squeezed orange juice
2-3 drops natural almond essence
1 tablespoon orange blossom water
6 egg yolks
100 g/4 oz sugar

5

125 g/5 oz ground almonds

1

1 Heat the oven to 180°C/350°F/Gas Mark 4.

2-3

2 In a small pan combine the orange juice, almond essence and orange blossom water. Bring to the boil and remove the pan from the heat.

3-5

3 In a mixer beat the yolks with the sugar for a minute or two until the mixture is pale and fluffy. Pour in the hot juice, add the ground almonds and mix well.

20-25

4 Divide the mixture between 6 small ramekins. Arrange the ramekins in a roasting pan and pour in boiling water to come halfway up the sides of the ramekins. Bake in the pre-heated oven for 20 minutes or until the custard is just set. Serve either hot or cold.

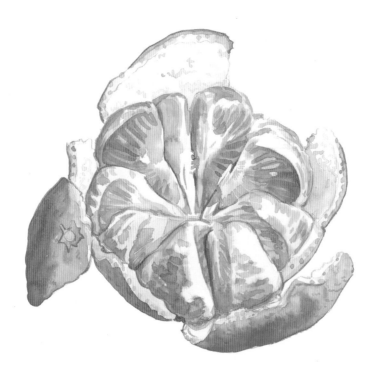

ALMOND CAKE WITH MANDARIN SYRUP

When winter sets in, the Mediterranean basin is literally awash with an amazing variety of citrus fruit. This pudding is wonderfully moist and fragrantly cake-like, making full use of the aromatic quality of those healthy, versatile fruits. Serve it either hot or cold accompanied by thick cream or, even better, with a large dollop of clotted cream. Serves 4.

30 minutes

150 g/6 oz softened butter
75 g/3 oz caster sugar
1 teaspoon grated orange peel
1 teaspoon grated lemon peel
3 eggs
150 g/6 oz ground almonds
3 tablespoons plain flour
a few drops of natural bitter almond essence
2 teaspoons orange blossom water
butter for greasing
2-3 tablespoons ground almonds or breadcrumbs

for the syrup
100 g/4 oz fresh mandarin or orange juice
½ teaspoon grated mandarin or orange peel
3 tablespoons good honey or sugar
2-3 tablespoons mandarin liqueur
mandarin segments for decoration

5

1

1 Heat the oven to 200°C/400°F/Gas Mark 6.

5

2 Place the softened butter and the sugar in the bowl of a food mixer and whisk at high speed for 3 minutes or until the butter is white and fluffy. Gradually add the rest of the ingredients and beat to a smooth cream.

17-22

3 Butter well a 23 cm/9 in flan dish, sprinkle with the ground almonds and knock out the excess. Pour the creamed mixture into the dish and spread it out evenly with a small spatula or the back of a spoon. Bake in the oven for 15-20 minutes or until set.

7-10

4 To make the syrup, combine the first three ingredients in a small sauce pan. Bring to the boil and simmer for about 5 minutes. Remove from the heat, cool slightly and add the liqueur. When the cake is cooked, pour the hot syrup over it, decorate with mandarin segments and serve from the flan dish, either hot or cold.

AVOCADO MOUSSE

A cool, pale green, refreshing and quick dessert given to me by Nira Rousso, an Israeli cook and food writer.

In Israel avocados are plentiful and a large variety appear in the market. One can find very large, pale green avocados with creamy pale yellow flesh, or smaller varieties, some smooth and green, some pimply and almost purple. There is even a small finger-like variety which does not have a stone. They are used, simply dressed with lemon juice, as a salad, mashed for sandwich fillings and dips or as an interesting addition to a fruit salad.

Although any ripe avocado will do, the most suitable for this recipe is the dark, rough-skinned variety which has a pronounced nutty flavour.

After cutting, avocado blackens very quickly. To prevent this, coat the exposed surface, with lemon juice immediately after cutting. Serves 4.

20 minutes

225 ml/8 fl.oz double cream, chilled
1 tablespoon sugar
1 teaspoon orange-blossom water
2 large ripe avocados, chilled
2 tablespoons good clear honey
3 tablespoons Grand Marnier or other orange liqueur
grated rind of 1 lime
juice of 2 limes

To decorate
zest of 1 lime, cut into julienne strips
sprigs of fresh mint

5

5

1 Whip the chilled cream until it forms soft but firm peaks. Add the sugar and orange-blossom water and mix well. Refrigerate.

5

2 Halve the avocados, remove the stones and scoop all the flesh into a food processor. Add all the remaining ingredients and process at high speed for 1 minute. Transfer to a mixing bowl and fold in the whipped cream.

3

3 Serve in individual glasses, each decorated with julienne of lime zest and a sprig of mint.

POMEGRANATES SERVED WITH CREAM

All around the Mediterranean the pomegranate is supposed to be a sacred fruit. In the Jewish tradition, it is said to have as many seeds as the number of good deeds the pious have to perform (start counting!). Crunching the seeds between your teeth is part of the fun of eating this exotic fruit.

The easiest way to peel a pomegranate is to remove its top and base, exposing the jewel-like red seed mass. Then, with a sharp knife, score through the outer peel so dividing the fruit into 4 segments. With your hands prise the peel from the delicate seeds, being careful to remove all traces of the thin yellow skin, which is very bitter. It sounds complicated but the whole process is rather quick and easy. It takes less than 5 minutes to prepare a fruit. Serves 4.

25 minutes

2 large pomegranates, prepared as above
500 g/1 lb crème fraîche or Greek yogurt, well chilled
50 g/2 oz granulated sugar
1 tablespoon orange blossom water or a few drops of vanilla extract
Grated zest of ½ lemon
25 g/1 oz flaked almonds

5

4 sprigs mint

10

1   Peel the pomegranates as described above.

1-2

2   Combine the crème fraîche or yogurt with the sugar, orange blossom water and the lemon zest, and mix well.

3   In each of 4 tall glasses arrange the pomegranate seed and cream mixture in alternate layers, finishing with

5

cream. Sprinkle with almonds, decorate with a sprig of mint and serve.

DEMIRHINDI SERBETI

This recipe came from Raphaela Lewis, one of the greatest authorities on everyday life in the Ottoman Empire. She tells a charming story about how the ice came to Istanbul from mountains situated hundreds of miles away: it was packed in thick felt cloth and first transported by a mule caravan, and then by sea until it finally arrived at the Sultan's table.

Now all you need for this surprisingly simple sorbet is a food processor and some ice cubes.

Make the sorbet immediately before serving. Other sweet syrups such as rose, mint or pomegranate cordial can also be used, in which case the addition of honey is unnecessary. Serves 6.

15 minutes

750 ml / 1½ pints ice cubes
a few drops of orange blossom water
4 tablespoons tamarind paste diluted with 100 ml / 4 fl. oz very cold water
4 tablespoons good runny honey
5
6 sprigs of mint

2-3   1 Put the ice into the food processor and process to a fine snow.

2   2 Divide the snow between 6 serving glasses and sprinkle with a few drops of orange blossom water.

3 Mix the tamarind paste with the honey. If it is too thick, dilute with a few drops of water. Pour this mixture
3-5   over the snow, decorate with mint sprigs and serve immediately.

STRAWBERRY & PEACH FRUIT SALAD IN RED WINE

15 minutes

Strawberries and red wine can be a surprising combination: make sure the berries are ripe and perfumed and the red wine fruity. Serves 4.

300 ml/10 fl.oz red wine
3 cloves, crushed
3 cardamom pods, crushed
1–2 tablespoons caster sugar
170 g/6 oz strawberries, hulled & halved
juice of 1 lemon

5

3 peaches, peeled, stoned & sliced

5

1 Heat one-third of the wine in a small pan with the cloves, cardamom and sugar. Simmer for a couple of minutes.

1

2 In a bowl mix the remaining wine with the lemon juice and strain into the spiced, cooked wine.

1

3 Add the prepared fruit and serve. This dish can also be served chilled.

SAUCES

HARISSA

This piquant and hot sauce is one of the most important flavourings of the north African kitchen. It is used to give fire to many dishes and will add flavour to mayonnaise, yogurt, cheese, pasta, rice or is delicious just mixed with butter and spread onto fresh bread. There are hundreds of recipes for harissa; some are mild, some fiery and some bordering on deadly! This one is hot – but not deadly.

The heat of the sauce is dictated by the heat of the chillies, which vary greatly. This recipe uses a combination of the large, not hot, red chillies (Westlands) and the very hot, small red chillies.

Use the harissa with discretion: first try adding one teaspoon and then progress until you reach a tolerable heat.

The quantity below makes about 500 g/1 lb, which seems a lot but the sauce will keep for up to 3 months, covered, in the fridge. Serves 4.

15 minutes

150 g/6 oz fresh red chillies (see above)
150 g/6 oz tomatoes, peeled & de-seeded
3 tablespoons tomato purée
7 large cloves of garlic, peeled
1 teaspoon ground cumin
50 ml/2 fl. oz vinegar
75 g/3 oz olive oil
1½ teaspoons salt

5

1   Remove the hard stems and de-seed the chillies. (For a hotter harissa, include the seeds.) Mince or process the chillies, tomatoes, tomato purée and garlic while adding the vinegar, oil and flavouring. Be careful to wash your hands very well after dealing with chillies.

8

2   Bottle in a glass jar. Cover with a thin layer of oil to prevent drying and seal tightly. The paste can be stored in the fridge for up to 3 months.

2

Harissa and
Salsa Verde (see page 265)

GREEN TAHINA SAUCE

Tahina is probably a Turkish invention but is used all over the Middle East, Greece, Egypt and North Africa. Tahina paste is a purée of sesame seeds which should first be diluted with water and lemon juice, then salt, garlic and parsley are added. It can be used as a dip or as a sauce with many dishes, such as falafel, fried aubergine or courgettes, or as a dressing for fresh salads. In Israel, this version is sometimes served as a dip for stuffed burgul dumplings. Serves 4.

5 minutes

100 g/4 oz raw tahina paste
juice of 1 lemon, or more
about 100 ml/4 fl.oz water
100 g/4 oz chopped fresh parsley, mint or dill

1–2 cloves of garlic
50 ml/2 fl.oz olive oil
salt

3

1 Put all the ingredients into a blender or food processor and process at high speed until a smooth sauce is achieved.

2

WALNUT TARATOR

An ancient Middle Eastern sauce which is still pungent and delicious today. It is traditionally served with fish or poultry but is suitable to accompany all kinds of vegetable. It is particularly good as an alternative dressing for salads, especially beetroot and apple salad. The sauce is very rich and the addition of chopped mint gives it an extra freshness. It will keep, covered, in the fridge for up to 1 week. Serves 4.

10 minutes

100 g/4 oz walnuts
4 cloves of garlic
2 slices of bread, crusts removed, soaked in water & squeezed dry
juice of 1–2 lemons
1/2 teaspoon grated lemon rind
salt
a few drops of tabasco
100 ml/4 fl.oz good olive oil
2 teaspoons chopped fresh mint, to garnish

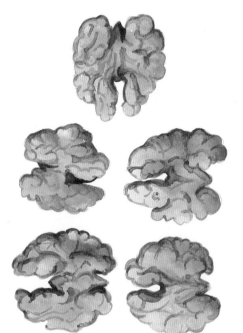

5

1 Put the walnuts into a food processor and process at high speed until powdered (about 1 minute). Add the garlic and the bread and process again until a smooth, thick cream is achieved. Add the lemon juice and rind, salt and tabasco and process for a further few seconds. With the processor on a high speed add the oil gradually, as for mayonnaise. Transfer to a serving bowl and sprinkle with the mint.

5 NOTE: The sauce can also be made with pine-nuts or hazelnuts.

YOGURT TARTAR

A multi-purpose, pleasantly tart sauce which is particularly delicious as a dressing for a warm potato salad. It can also be served as a dip for cooked asparagus, artichokes or leeks. Although named after the Tartars, the fierce warriors who roamed the steppes of Asia, the idea for the sauce comes from the gentle and sophisticated French kitchen.

You can vary the sauce by using lemon grass, pickled gherkin or garlic instead of or as well as the capers. Serves 4–6.

10 minutes

350 g/12 oz Greek yogurt
1 teaspoon mustard powder
1 teaspoon salt
juice of 1 lemon or lime

5

½ teaspoon grated lemon or lime rind

50 ml/2 fl.oz olive oil
75 g/3 oz gherkin, finely chopped
3 oz/75 g shallots, finely chopped
50 g/2 oz capers, either whole or roughly chopped

5

1   Combine the yogurt, mustard, salt and lemon or lime juice and rind in a bowl and mix well. Add the oil gradually, beating all the time. Add the remaining ingredients, stirring well to combine. Refrigerate.

YOGURTTESE (YOGURT MAYONNAISE)

A lighter and therefore 'slimmer' version of traditional mayonnaise. Although hazelnut oil is rather expensive it gives the sauce an exquisite, fragrant, nutty flavour. Ideal to use as a dip for asparagus, leeks or artichokes.

You can add some garlic and/or mustard to give the sauce bite. Like mayonnaise, it is best made by hand, which will take about 6–7 minutes or – much quicker and almost as good – in a food processor, which will take 1 minute. The sauce will keep for up to a week, covered, at the bottom of the fridge. Serves 6–8.

10 minutes

200 g/7 oz Greek yogurt
200 g/7 oz fromage frais
1 teaspoon mustard powder (optional)

2

juice of 1 lemon

½ teaspoon grated lemon rind
100 ml/4 fl.oz hazelnut oil
salt & freshly ground black pepper

1   In a bowl combine the yogurt, fromage frais, mustard, if used, and lemon juice and rind. Add a few drops of oil and beat until amalgamated. Continue pouring in the oil and beating, as for mayonnaise, until all the oil is used. The sauce should now be glossy and thick enough to coat a spoon. Season with salt and pepper. Refrigerate in

5-8

the bottom part of the fridge.

Alternatively, combine all the ingredients except the oil in a food processor, switch to high speed and add the oil

2

in a steady stream.

TAPENADE

This delicious sauce encapsulates the flavour of the Mediterranean. Its origin is in the South of France and its name comes from the old Provençal word for capers – tapeno. Traditionally the sauce is made with a pestle and mortar which does not take much time but it involves experience and much elbow grease. Making it in the processor will take about 2 minutes but the texture is much too fine.

Most of the available stoned olives are, at best, tasteless. Therefore do buy good olives which, unfortunately, usually come with the stone. Stoning olives can be made easy with a special olive stoner. These are readily available in many kitchen equipment stores.

Tapenade is a versatile sauce. It is served as a dip with raw vegetables, as a spread on crusty bread or try it together with plenty of fresh herbs as a quick sauce for pasta. It keeps in the fridge for up to a month. **Serves 4.**

20 minutes

2 heaped tablespoons capers, drained
1 x 50 g/2 oz tin of anchovies, drained
250 g/8 oz good black olives, stoned
4 tablespoons virgin olive oil
5
a few drops of lemon juice

10-15 by hand
or 3-4 by
machine

1   Either put the capers and anchovies into a pestle and pound into a paste. Then add the olives a few at the time and pound until completely crushed. Add the olive oil, a little at a time, like making mayonnaise and pound until all the oil is absorbed and the mixture is homogenous. Add the lemon juice and mix well. Or, put the first 3 ingredients into the processor and process for 1 minute. While the machine is running add the oil in a thin steady stream, add the lemon juice and mix well. Cover and refrigerate.

NOTE: The anchovy marinating oil, especially if it is olive oil, can be added to the sauce. Remember to reduce the total quantity of oil accordingly.

AVGOLEMONO

Avgolemono is an egg and lemon sauce, an extremely versatile one suitable for fish, poultry and many vegetables such as plainly boiled asparagus, courgettes and globe artichokes. It is especially good with boiled chicken. The sauce, which is basically a savoury custard, is easy to make but be very careful not to overheat as the sauce, like any egg custard, can curdle easily. **Serves 4.**

15 minutes

4 egg yolks
100 ml/4 fl. oz lemon juice (or to taste)
½ teaspoon grated lemon zest
250 ml/8 fl. oz hot chicken stock
2
salt

5

1   Whisk the yolks until pale and frothy (about 2 minutes in a mixer at high speed). Add the lemon juice and zest and mix well. Whisk in the hot stock.

2   Transfer the mixture into the top of a double boiler, reduce the heat to minimum, and cook mixing all the time for about 4-5 minutes or until the sauce is just thick enough to coat a spoon. The sauce can be served either hot or cold.

7-10

LEMON GRASS & CHILLI SAUCE

A fragrant hot chilli sauce of Thai origin. Use for dipping steamed vegetables and fried kuftas (patties). It is also delicious poured over hot or cold boiled rice, making it savoury and more interesting. Lemon grass is becoming available in more and more supermarkets, and rightly so. It is also readily available in many oriental shops. Do not be tempted to use dried lemon grass as it is entirely different and suitable only for making a pleasant herbal tea. Serves 4.

4 minutes

100 ml/4 fl.oz light soy sauce
50 ml/2 fl.oz dark soy sauce
50 g/2 oz lemon grass, chopped
2 red chillies, thinly sliced
75 ml/3 fl. oz rice or white wine vinegar
50 ml/2 fl. oz Chinese sesame oil
1 teaspoon sugar

1 Mix all the ingredients together in a bowl.

NOTE: More chilli can be used if a hotter sauce is preferred.

LEMON & GARLIC SAUCE

A great classic sauce used all around the Mediterranean and anywhere lemons grow, where it is used to baste fried and grilled fish and poultry, or as a dip for vegetable fritters or plain fresh vegetables. Simply pour it over a mound of hot burgul or rice for a quick and light main course. Serves 6–8.

5 minutes

juice of 2–3 lemons
150 ml/5 fl.oz good fruity olive oil
2–3 cloves of garlic, crushed & mashed with a little salt
4 tablespoons chopped fresh parsley
4 tablespoons chopped fresh dill

2–3 green or red chillies or some chilli powder (optional)
1 teaspoon sugar (optional)
salt
2–3 tablespoons water

1 In a bowl mix together all the ingredients except the water. Dilute the sauce to taste with the water.

GARLIC SAUCE

Garlic is one of the basic ingredients in the Mediterranean kitchen. The flavour of garlic changes as it cooks. Fresh garlic is pungent and hot in flavour while stewed garlic has an elusive, delicate perfume and has an exquisite melt-in-the-mouth texture. A sweet garlic preserve is often made in southern Italy. The sauce below belongs to a vast family of garlic sauces and is a bit less oily and therefore healthier than the French Aïoli. It is delicious served as a dip for fresh vegetables or to accompany grilled fish or meat.

The use of bread instead of egg yolks as an emulsifying agent is ancient. Soaked bread absorbs oil and makes a sauce with a texture similar to mayonnaise. This simple technique is especially important in a cholesterol-free diet. Include some fresh herbs in the sauce which add a lot of lightness to the intense garlic flavour. Serves 4.

15 minutes

> *100 g/4 oz good white bread, crust removed, soaked in water*
> *1 head of garlic (about 6-8 cloves), peeled*
> *juice of 1 lemon*
> *grated zest of ½ lemon*
> *250 ml/8 fl.oz olive oil*
> *2 tablespoons chopped parsley (optional)*

5

1 Squeeze the bread dry and put it into a food processor, together with all the other ingredients except the olive oil.

1

2 Process to a smooth cream. Add the oil in a thin steady stream while the machine is running, like making mayonnaise. The sauce can be kept for up to a week, in the fridge, in a tightly covered container.

3-5

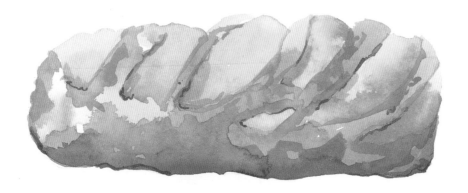

SALSA VERDE

This bright green and pungent sauce appears all over the Mediterranean. It is delicious served with grilled fish or grilled chicken. Serve it as a dressing on potato salad or just poured over burgul or rice as a light main course. Serves 4.

15 minutes

50 g/2 oz crustless white bread, soaked in water
1 large bunch of flat-leaf parsley, stems removed
75 g/3 oz sorrel or spinach, washed well
25 g/1 oz capers
50 g/2 oz anchovy fillet
1 hard boiled egg
2 tablespoons white wine vinegar

5
100 ml/4 fl.oz/½ cup olive oil

1
1   Squeeze the bread dry and put it together with the rest of the ingredients, except the oil, into a food processor. Process into a smooth cream.

2   With the machine running, add the oil in a slow, steady stream, like making mayonnaise. Process for a few seconds until the sauce is smooth and creamy. Refrigerate covered,

8
until required.

SALSA

10-20 minutes

A deliciously piquant sauce of Mexican origin. It can be served both hot or cold and can be used as a dip as well as a sauce. Toss it with hot pasta for a substantial main course. The sauce will keep for up to 2 weeks, tightly sealed, in the fridge. Serves 4.

1 large onion, coarsely chopped
2 cloves of garlic
100 g/4 oz sweet red pepper, chopped
100 g/4 oz sweet green pepper, chopped
100 g/4 oz yellow pepper, chopped
50 g/2 oz red or green chillies, chopped
50 ml/2 fl.oz olive, corn or peanut oil

3 tablespoons red wine or sherry vinegar
salt
1 teaspoon sugar (optional)
100 g/4 oz firm tomatoes, peeled & finely chopped
2 tablespoons chopped fresh coriander leaves

5

1   Put all the ingredients except the tomato and coriander leaves into a food processor and process, starting and stopping the machine until the mixture is finely chopped but not puréed. The sauce should look like a finely chopped salad. Add the tomato together with the coriander leaves, mix well and chill.

For a smoother version: process all the above ingredients except the coriander. Transfer the sauce from the food processor to a small saucepan, bring to the boil, then simmer for 10 minutes. Return to the processor with the tomato and process until smooth (about 1 minute at high speed). Pass through a sieve and serve either hot or cold, adding the chopped coriander just before serving.

5-15

NOTE: When dealing with chillies it is important to remember that the seeds, the hottest part, can cause real damage to sensitive skin, or to the eyes and nose. Either wear gloves to chop chillies or wash your hands thoroughly after handling them.

FRESH TOMATO SAUCE

15 minutes

A quick and easy uncooked tomato sauce with a delicate pink colour and the full flavour of fresh tomatoes. The best tomatoes to use are either fully ripe Italian plum or Provençale tomatoes. The sauce is delicious with fried, grilled or steamed vegetables, and even as a cooling agent with a dry, hot curry. Serves 6–8.

500 g/1 lb 2 oz tomatoes, roughly chopped
1 clove of garlic, chopped
1 teaspoon salt
2 tablespoons lemon juice
grated rind of ½ lemon

a few drops of tabasco
100 ml/4 fl.oz good olive oil
1–2 tablespoons chopped fresh basil, tarragon or mint
   (optional)

2

1   Put the tomatoes into a blender or a food processor and process at high speed for 1 minute. Pass the resulting pulp through a sieve. Add the garlic, salt, lemon juice, lemon rind and tabasco and mix well. Beat in the oil gradually, as for mayonnaise. Either serve plain or flavoured with chopped herbs.

10-12

Clockwise from the top:
Fresh Tomato Sauce; Salsa; Yogurttese;
Green Tahina Sauce; Walnut Tarator

ROUGH TOMATO SAUCE

It is difficult to imagine the Mediterranean kitchen without tomatoes, considering that in many places the common use of the tomato started as late as the beginning of this century.

There is nothing more delicious then a local Mediterranean tomato, be they the fleshy Italian plum tomatoes that are essential for a good, full-bodied sauce or the slightly minty, sweet, big tomatoes sold in every local market. The tart sweetness of the tomato makes an ideal combination with olive oil, garlic and onion thus making the tomato the base for many sauces. The following are two versions of tomato sauce: the first a rough, mild sauce that goes very well with pasta or meat balls; the second, a smooth, spicy sauce that goes well with fish or chicken. Made thick enough, these sauces can be used as dips. Serves 4.

30 minutes

5 tablespoons virgin olive oil
2 medium onions, peeled & roughly chopped
3-4 fat cloves of garlic, peeled & roughly chopped
3 celery stems, finely chopped
1 kg / 2 lb Italian plum tomatoes, peeled, de-seeded & roughly chopped
1 tablespoon tomato purée
a large bouquet garni composed of a few twigs of thyme or oregano,
*   flat parsley, celery leaves & a strip or two of orange zest*
salt & freshly ground black pepper

10

3

1 Heat the oil in a heavy-based frying pan, add the onion, garlic and celery and fry, over high heat, stirring until the onion starts to change colour.

2 Add the rest of the ingredients and fry for a few minutes mixing all the time. Reduce the heat to minimum and simmer, uncovered for about 15 minutes; stir frequently to avoid scorching. If you prefer a smoother sauce, remove the bouquet garni, transfer into a food processor and process until smooth.

17-20

SPICY TOMATO SAUCE

30 minutes

4 tablespoons virgin olive oil
2 medium onions, peeled & roughly chopped
3-4 fat cloves of garlic, peeled & crushed
1-2 or more red chillies or ½ teaspoon or more good chilli powder (to taste)
1 fennel bulb, outer leaves discarded, chopped
1 scant teaspoon fennel seeds
1 kg/2 lb Italian plum tomatoes, peeled, de-seeded & roughly chopped
1 tablespoon tomato purée
4 anchovy fillets, roughly chopped

5

salt & freshly ground black pepper

1   Heat the oil in a heavy-based frying pan, add the onion, garlic, chilli, fennel and fennel seeds. Fry for a few minutes, stirring, until the onion starts to be transparent. Add the tomatoes, the purée and the anchovy and continue to fry, over high heat, for a minute or two. Season to taste. Reduce the heat to minimum and simmer, uncovered, for 15 minutes.

18-20

2   Transfer the cooked mixture to a processor and process at high speed until the required texture is achieved. Return to the frying pan and re-heat. The sauce can be kept in the fridge, covered, for up to a week.

3

NOTE: To de-seed tomatoes, cut peeled tomatoes in half and squeeze out the seeds.

SALSA AGRO-DOLCE

25 minutes

This sweet and sour sauce originated in the kitchens of the Roman Empire and is still used today all over the Mediterranean. It can be served instead of the traditional gravy with roast lamb or venison and makes an interesting base for meat balls or chicken ragù. Serves 4.

2 medium onions, peeled
2 tablespoons pine-nuts
4 tablespoons olive oil
250 ml/8 fl. oz chicken stock
2 tablespoons honey
100 g/4 oz seedless raisins
1 tablespoon cornflour
4 tablespoons good red wine or sherry vinegar
salt
3   *2 tablespoons chopped mint (optional)*

2

1 Place the onion and pine nuts in the food processor and process at high speed until the mixture is chopped but not puréed.

15

2 Heat the oil in a heavy-based frying pan. Add the onion and nut mixture and fry for about 5 minutes or until nicely golden. Add the stock, honey and raisins. Reduce the heat and simmer gently for 10 minutes.

3-5

3 Dissolve the cornflour in the vinegar and add to the cooking sauce and simmer for a few minutes more. Add the salt and mint and serve hot, with cold meats or hot, roasted lamb or venison.

NOTE: To use as cooking sauce: bring the sauce to simmering point and add the meat; continue to simmer for about 25-30 minutes or until meat is cooked.

GREEN CHILLI AND CORIANDER SAUCE

10 minutes

This fiery, fragrant sauce originated in the Yemen where it is popular served with soups, and meat and fish dishes, or is simply used as a piquant dip for bread and raw vegetables. Serves 4.

250 g/8 oz green chillies, cored & de-seeded
5 fat cloves of garlic, peeled
large bunch of coriander leaves, trimmed
2 teaspoons coriander seeds
½ teaspoon black pepper
½ teaspoon clove
6 cardamom pods
1½ teaspoons salt
3   *oil*

5

1 Place the chillies, garlic and coriander in a food processor and process, starting and stopping the machine until the mixture is finely chopped but not puréed. Place the spices and the salt in a coffee grinder or a spice mill and grind to a fine powder. Mix well with the processed ingredients.

2

2 Pack into clean, sterile jars, cover with a thin layer of oil. Stored in the refrigerator, this spicy sauce can last for up to a month.

CUCUMBER AND YOGURT SAUCE

25 minutes

The following recipe is based on tsatsiki, a Balkan classic which probably originated in Turkey. It is refreshingly cooling and can be used to accompany fish and chicken dishes, used as a dressing for salads or simply as a dip for raw vegetables and other dishes. Serves 4.

2 large cucumbers, washed well
350 ml/12 fl oz strained, Greek-style yogurt
4 cloves of garlic, mashed with a little salt
3 tablespoons fruity olive oil
juice of a small lemon
salt & freshly ground pepper
5   *4-5 tablespoons finely chopped mint or flat parsley*

1 Place the cucumber in a food processor and process, starting and stopping the machine until the mixture is finely chopped but not puréed. Transfer into a bowl, sprinkle with some salt and leave for 15 minutes. Strain,
20   discard the liquid, rinse well and squeeze the pulp dry.

2   2 Add the rest of the ingredients and mix well. The sauce will keep covered in a refrigerator for up to a week.

QUICK APRICOT 'JAM' SAUCE

This is based on a recipe of Anton Mosimann, a superbly creative chef who takes into account not only the taste and appearance of a dish but also its nutritional value. It is light and refreshing and keeps for up to a week, covered, in the fridge. It can also be frozen for up to 2 months, but freezing will affect the texture.

The hazelnuts are used to give the 'jam' body and texture. Raw nuts can be used but to get a fuller flavour, roast them lightly. The 'jam' can be served immediately after making but improves if left for a few hours.

The same method can be used for oranges, plums, peaches, nectarines and blueberries. Remember to adjust the sweetness and liqueur according to the fruit used. Orange 'jam' is delicious with the addition of 1 tablespoon lightly roasted, crushed coriander seeds. Serves 4.

20 minutes

Makes about 500 g/1 lb

500 g/1 lb 2 oz fresh apricots
75 g/3 oz hazelnuts
4 tablespoons clear honey
1 teaspoon grated lemon rind
juice of 1 lemon
2–3 tablespoons apricot brandy or cognac

5

10

1 Halve the apricots and remove the stones. Crack 5 of the stones, remove the kernels and chop them finely. Taste the kernels; if too bitter use only one or two. Put the chopped kernels and hazelnuts into a food processor and process at high speed for 1 minute.

3-5

2 Add the remaining ingredients and continue to process at high speed, starting and stopping the machine, until the fruit is chopped but not puréed.

REAL EGG CUSTARD SAUCE

There is nothing like a real egg custard. It is smooth, velvety and, if flavoured correctly, a superb accompaniment to any dessert. It can be served either hot or cold. Cold egg custard flavoured with good cognac or Grand Marnier is my favourite accompaniment to traditional Christmas pudding. Serves 4.

30 minutes

300 ml/10 fl.oz milk
150 ml/5 fl.oz double cream
4 scented geranium leaves (optional)
2 strips of lemon zest
2 teaspoons orange-blossom water or 1 vanilla pod
6 egg yolks (size 3)
2 tablespoons caster sugar

2

8

1 In a small, heavy-based saucepan mix the milk and cream, add the geranium leaves, lemon zest and orange-blossom water or vanilla pod and bring to the boil. Reduce the heat and simmer very gently for 5 minutes.

2 In a bowl combine the egg yolks and sugar and beat until pale and fluffy. Strain the milk and pour it over the eggs, beating constantly. Return the custard to the pan and cook over a very low heat, stirring all the time and never allowing the custard to boil, until thick enough to coat a spoon. Or, which takes longer but is much safer, place the pan in a larger pan containing simmering water and cook for about 10–15 minutes, stirring all the time until thick enough to coat a spoon. Serve either hot or cold.

20

RASPBERRY SAUCE

This extremely quick and easy sauce goes very well with both hot and cold sweets. You can make a sauce in the same way with strawberries, blackberries or Cape gooseberries. When using strawberries I sometimes add about 2 teaspoons chopped fresh mint – Eau de Cologne, pineapple or common garden mint – to enhance the flavour. The sauce will keep for 3–4 days, covered, in the fridge. Serves 6–8.

5 minutes

500 g/1 lb 2 oz raspberries
3 tablespoons clear honey
juice of 1 small lemon

1

1 Put all the ingredients except the lemon rind into a food processor and process at high speed for 1 minute. Pass through a sieve, add the lemon rind, mix and refrigerate.

4

CLEAR VEGETABLE STOCK

Good stock is the foundation of all good food, adding savour and depth to any dish. The following is light, fragrant and golden in colour. You can vary the flavouring by changing the ingredients of the bouquet garni, adding different herbs, lemon grass or orange, etc. In the autumn also add 100 g/4 oz chopped pumpkin.

Using stock is especially important when cooking vegetables, so please do not omit it. At a pinch, stock cubes can be used as a substitute but generally they are too salty and with a dominant celery flavour. This stock will keep for up to a week, covered, in the fridge. Serves 4.

30 minutes

Makes 850 ml/1¼ pints

> *1 large onion, sliced into rings*
> *100 g/4 oz carrots, washed well & sliced*
> *100 g/4 oz pumpkin (in season)*
> *4 sticks of celery, sliced*
> *1 large ripe tomato, quartered*
> *1 bouquet garni, made from 4 sprigs of parsley,*
>   *4 sprigs of coriander leaves, 2 sprigs of thyme*
>   *and 2 strips of lemon zest, tied in a piece of string*
> *1 teaspoon black peppercorns*

5

> *1.5 litres/3 pints water*

25

1 Put all the ingredients into a large saucepan.
    Bring to the boil, then simmer for 25 minutes. Strain.

QUICK CHICKEN STOCK

You probably wonder what a recipe for chicken stock is doing in a book which deals with fast food. The reason is that especially in fast cooking stock is an essential ingredient. It gives soups, sauces and stews the depth of flavour and texture which normally take long and slow cooking to achieve.

Making stock properly, although not technically complicated, takes a long time – with the help of a pressure cooker the cooking process takes only 20-25 minutes. Although not as clear or as refined, pressure cooking produces stock that can give body to otherwise thin and anaemic dishes. For extra body condense the stock by boiling it rapidly until reduced by half or even more. Fresh stock will last, covered, in the fridge for up to 2 weeks. It can also be frozen successfully for up to 3 months. Serves 4.

30 minutes

1 medium chicken (about 1½ kg/3 lb), cut into portions
2 large carrots, washed & coarsely chopped
1 large unpeeled onion, washed well & roughly sliced
3 celery sticks, roughly chopped
2 small tomatoes, halved
100 g/4 oz of pumpkin or 1-2 courgettes
A bouquet garni made with a few sprigs of thyme, parsley, 2 bay leaves
*   & a small strip of lemon or orange peel*
4 cloves
½ teaspoon peppercorns
2.5 cm/1 in piece of cinnamon stick (optional)
water to cover (about 1.5 litres/3 pints)

5

1   Place all the above ingredients in the pressure cooker. Cover with water, being careful not to exceed the manufacturer's recommendation. Cover tightly and bring to pressure (15 lb gauge). Reduce the heat and simmer, under pressure, for 20 minutes.

25

2   Remove the cooker from the heat and reduce the pressure under cold water. Strain the liquid. The stock can be used as required.

2

NOTE: The cooked chicken meat, mixed with potatoes and other cooked vegetables and served with garlic sauce (see page 264), makes an interesting salad.

FISH STOCK

Fish stock gives soups and stews much of their richness and individuality. The short time required to cook the fish is not enough for the gravy to develop depth of flavour. Making fish stock is quick and easy and the stock can be kept covered in the fridge for up to a week. It can be successfully frozen and kept for up to 3 months.

When buying fish ask also for extra skin and bones; most good fishmongers will gladly oblige. Try to avoid using the skins or bones of oily fish such as mackerel; white fish, trout and salmon make a good well balanced stock. If you prefer stock flavoursome always include a red mullet with the fish head and bones which impart a delicious gamey aroma to the stock. Serves 4.

30 minutes

1 kg/2 lb fish skin & bones
1 small red mullet (optional)
1 large onion, peeled & sliced
2 carrots, washed & sliced
1 fennel, washed & sliced
Bouquet garni made of a few stems & leaves of parsley & celery, a small sprig of thyme,
*   a strip of lemon zest & 1-2 bay leaves*
1/2 teaspoon black peppercorns
1/2 teaspoons fennel seeds (optional)
water to cover (or a mixture of water & white wine)

6

3

1   Wash the fish heads, bones and skin in a few changes of cold water and lay them on the bottom of a large, heavy-based pot.

20-25

2   Add the rest of the ingredients and cover with cold water. Bring to the boil, reduce the heat and simmer, very gently, for 20-25 minutes. Strain the liquid and use as needed.

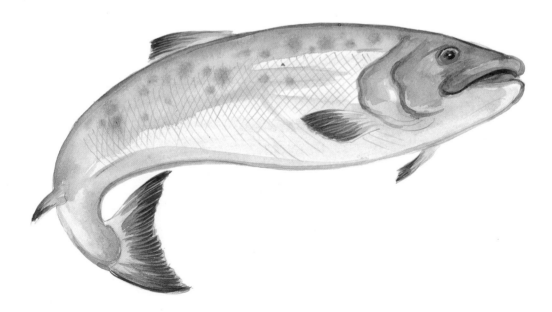

EASY MEAT STOCK

At one time or another we all face this situation – we start to cook and only then realise that we are out of stock. The answer is to have a supply of stock cubes. With a few simple additions these can be made into a rather delicious base for soups and stews. Serves 4.

40 minutes

2 tablespoons mild olive or ground nut oil
1 large onion with the skin left on, washed & coarsely chopped
1 clove of garlic, coarsely chopped
2 carrots, coarsely chopped
a small bulb of fennel, coarsely chopped
3 stalks of celery, coarsely chopped
2-3 red tomatoes, sliced
bouquet garni: 2-3 bay leaves, celery leaves, parsley leaves & stalks, fresh thyme & marjoram,
  & a few strips of lemon peel
1.4 litre (2½ pts) water or water and white wine

5

2-3 good stock cubes

1 Heat the oil in a large, heavy-based pan. Add the vegetables and fry over a high heat for about 5 minutes or until they start to colour. Add the rest of the ingredients and bring to a boil. Reduce the heat and simmer for 25 minutes.

30

5

2 Strain and use. The stock can be kept for a few days, covered in a refrigerator.

Index